The ENCYCLOPEDIA of
— DEER —

Your Guide to the World's Deer Species,
Including Whitetails, Mule Deer,
Caribou, Elk, Moose, and More

Dr. Leonard Lee Rue III

Voyageur Press

Edited by Amy Rost-Holtz
Designed by Maria Friedrich
Printed in China

03 04 05 06 07 5 4 3 2 1

Library of Congress Cataloging-in-Publication Data

Rue, Leonard Lee.
  The encyclopedia of deer : your guide to the world's deer species including whitetails, mule deer, caribou, elk, moose, and more / Leonard Lee Rue III.
     p. cm.
Includes bibliographical references and index.
  ISBN 0-89658-590-5 (hardcover)
  1. Cervidae—Encyclopedias. 2. Musk deer—Encyclopedias. I. Title.
  QL737.U55R825 2004
  599.65'03—dc22
                                    2003018646

Distributed in Canada by Raincoast Books,
9050 Shaughnessy Street, Vancouver, B.C. V6P 6E5

Published by Voyageur Press, Inc.
123 North Second Street, P.O. Box 338,
Stillwater, MN 55082 U.S.A.
651-430-2210, fax 651-430-2211
books@voyageurpress.com
www.voyageurpress.com

Page 1: This red deer stag would be called "royal" because of the crown-like cluster of tines on the end of his main beams. (Photograph by Leonard Lee Rue III)

Page 2: A whitetail doe peers cautiously through the foliage. (Photograph by Uschi Rue)

Page 3, top left: The Shiras is the smallest of moose subspecies. This bull shows the characteristic "basket" curve of the antler palms and tines. (Photograph by Leonard Lee Rue III)

Page 3, bottom left: The large antlers on this mule deer buck shows the bifurcation, or branching, of the main beams. (Photograph by Len Rue Jr.)

Page 3, right: Of all the world's deer, the fallow deer is probably the one recognized by the greatest number of people. A native of southern Europe and the eastern Mediterranean, it has been imported into other parts of Europe, as well as North and South America, Asia, Australia, and New Zealand. (Photograph by Leonard Lee Rue III)

Page 4: Resplendent in his new winter coat, this magnificent bull elk tends a cow during rutting season. Just the size of his antlers and body is enough to deter most rivals. (Photograph by Uschi Rue)

Page 5: Sika deer are also known as Japanese deer, because *sika* means *deer* in Japanese. (Photograph by Leonard Lee Rue III)

Page 8: This is one of the largest barren-ground caribou bulls ever photographed. (Photograph by Leonard Lee Rue III)

DEDICATION

This book is dedicated to my cousins. Among the Sellners: John "Jackie" Sellner; Florence "Dolly" Fritz; Patricia Merlo; Harold Sellner; Edith Mae Walls; Robert Sellner; Carole Mae Sellner; Lynn Wilson; Nancy Allan.

Among the Rues: William Murray; James Murray; Alice Carey Bailey; Nina Warren Beauchamp; Margaret Warren Williams; Thomas Bruce Warren; Elinor Warren Roberts.

ACKNOWLEDGMENTS

Although my study of deer began sixty-three years ago, on a June morning in 1939, it has been a lifetime occupation with no end in sight. I live with, work with, and study deer almost every day of my life, and I still get the feeling that I have more to learn than what I have learned. This is the sixth book I have written about deer, and none of them could have been written if I had not, in addition to my own lifetime of experience, had access to the lifetime of knowledge of the many men and women who have also devoted their lives to the study of deer. I hereby acknowledge my debt to all of the authors listed in the bibliography. However, I want to single out G. Kenneth Whitehead of England and Dr. Valerius Geist of Canada for special thanks.

I want to thank my secretary, Marilyn Maring, for translating my handwriting into a typed manuscript that can be read. I want to thank my son, Len Rue Jr., for the use of some of his photos.

As always, it was a pleasure to work with my editor at Voyageur Press, Amy Rost-Holtz. We are on the same wavelength, and it helps.

I especially want to thank my lovely wife, Uschi, for her constant support of me and everything I do.

Dr. Leonard Lee Rue III

CONTENTS

INTRODUCTION

How many species of deer are there in the world? That's a good question and one that is most difficult to answer because even the taxonomists—the biologists that classify the species—don't agree. Taxonomy has never been set in concrete—classifications are constantly changing, because ongoing mitochondrial DNA testing is applied to all animals. The answer can vary depending upon which scientific reports and books you read. For the purposes of this book, there are forty-six species in the *Cervidae* family, and if you add the five species in the *Moschidae* family, as most taxonomists do, there are fifty-one species total.

What is a species? A species basically is an organism, in this case an animal, in which the individuals are similar in form and function and are capable of breeding, combining genes, and producing fertile offspring. Some species are capable of interbreeding but are prevented from so doing because of physical barriers to their ranges or because they are not keyed into the courtship patterns of other species. Some species do interbreed but their offspring are handicapped because they do not inherit the best traits of either species. Still other species interbreed but their offspring are infertile.

A truly fine example of a white-tailed buck. (Photograph by Uschi Rue)

For most species, the fact that they can't interbreed guarantees that the eons of evolution and natural selection that produced the species will not be wasted. Most of the animal species living today are specialists that evolved to survive best in the niche in which they are found. Some species are highly adaptable and are able to increase both their numbers and their ranges. Other species are so habitat- or food-selective that they cannot adapt to changing conditions and thus are pushed ever closer to extinction.

To better understand how a species as small as a northern pudu, standing 12 inches (305 mm) high at the shoulder, is distantly related to an Alaskan-Yukon moose, standing 91.6 inches (2,350 mm) high at the shoulder, we need to know how species are classified. For example, the chart below shows how each of these species is scientifically classified.

A subspecies is often derived from the fact that the individual animals in one geographic location are different in size, coloration, and cranial measurements than their counterparts in other, often more isolated, locations. Humans often introduce subspecies from one area into others, in order to re-establish a subspecies that has been decimated or in an effort to produce larger specimens. Where the ranges of two subspecies overlap, the subspecies can and do interbreed. At times, the outward physical differences between the subspecies are so slight that only DNA. testing can distinguish one from another.

There is considerable confusion about the proper terms to be used for the gender of deer. It began more than a thousand years ago, when royalty reserved for itself the exclusive right to shoot the larger members of the deer family. The males of the animals classified as *Cervus*, such as the red deer (*Cervus elaphus*), reindeer (*Rangifer tarandus*), and European moose (*Alces alces*), were called stags. The females were called hinds and the young were referred to as calves. The males of the lesser animals that could be hunted by common folk, including the fallow and roe deer (*Dama dama*

and *Capreolus capreolus*), were called bucks. The females were called does and the young were called fawns. And it's still that way today.

In North America male elk (*Cervus elaphus canadensis*), caribou (*Rangifer tarandus*), and moose (*Alces alces*) are referred to as bulls. Females are called cows and the young are called calves. The males of all other members of the deer family are called bucks, the females are called does, and the young are called fawns.

The young of most members of the deer family are referred to as "hiders," because their mothers hide them in dense vegetation for the first one to two weeks of their lives. Most does establish birthing territories from which they exclude all other members of their own species. To avoid detection by predators, the young depend on their cryptic coloration, their lack of scent, their ability to remain motionless, and the fact that their mothers ingest their feces and urine.

Most deer are solitary creatures or members of small family groups; they herd only under certain feeding conditions or during migration. The main exceptions are the caribou and reindeer, who constantly live and travel in herds. Their young, by necessity, are "followers." While the herd does slow down during the birthing period, it still has to keep moving to obtain new forage. Newborn caribou and reindeer are standing and walking within minutes of their birth, so they can follow after their mothers as they rejoin the moving herd.

It is possible to determine the age of wild animals by examining in a laboratory the layers of cementium deposits in their teeth, but this is expensive and time consuming, and so is not often done. This book gives the maximum age recorded for captive animals of different species, because it is largely from captive animals that we have any idea of how long an animal might live. Captive animals, however, are usually kept under carefully monitored conditions, and that allows an animal to reach its greatest potential. Even under the most favorable conditions, it would be unusual

	Alaska-Yukon Moose	Northern Pudu	
1 Kingdom	Animalia	Animalia	Animals
2 Phylum	Chordata	Chordata	Having a backbone
3 Class	Mammalia	Mammalia	Having mammary glands and nursing its young
4 Order	Artiodactyla	Artiodactyla	Having an even number of toes on each foot
5 Family	*Cervidae*	*Cervidae*	Deer family
6 Genus	*Alces*	*Pudu*	
7 Species	*Alces gigas*	*Mephistophiles*	

The proper terms for the sexes of deer vary by species and where the deer are found. For example, the male white-tailed deer is called a buck, the female is a doe, and the young are called fawns (top photo). For moose and elk (wapiti), a male is called a bull, the female is called a cow, and the young are called calves (middle photos). In Eurasia, the males of the red deer family are called stags, the females are called hinds, and the young are called calves (left). (Photographs by Leonard Lee Rue III)

for a wild creature to live half as long as the ages given for captive animals. In the wild, fully 40 percent of wild creatures die or are killed before they are one year old.

The order in which the species are discussed in this book follows the pattern used in scientific texts and journals, based on the species' placement on the evolutionary time scale. The earliest deer had little tusks, or canine teeth, which they used as defensive weapons. As time passed, deer became larger in body size, their tusks became smaller, and small antlers grew on their heads. Gradually, the deer and their antlers became much larger, and the tusks all but disappeared in later species. (However, rudimentary teeth are still found in some, such as the white-tailed deer and the elk [wapiti].)

The information given for each species includes:
❖ Range;
❖ Description of the animal and its physical characteristics, such as glands and antlers or tusks;
❖ Habits, including habitat and adaptation to it, food, socialization, and migration behavior;
❖ Communication, including chemical, visual, and vocal methods of communicating;
❖ Breeding seasons and habits;
❖ Birth and young, including the timing of births during the year and the number of young;

❖ Enemies, which may include parasites, animals, or humans; and
❖ Relationship with humans, describing how humans may use, or otherwise have an impact on the life of the deer.

The information is much more comprehensive for some species than for others. For instance, many people are interested in and have seen the white-tailed deer, and it is heavily hunted. Researchers have responded by making it the most extensively studied deer in the world. Other species, such as barasingha, marsh deer, and huemuls, are seldom seen and are close to extinction in the wild; most such species are not represented in zoo collections. The dearth of information available on them corresponds with the lack of human interest. (For more information on the rare species given in this basic text, consult the books listed in the bibliography.)

However, the lesser known *Cervidae* species exhibit many of the same behaviors as their more recognizable cousins. Studying the physical features and habits of such species as whitetails, mule deer, elk (wapiti), and caribou gives a basis for comparison and thus gives insight into the lives of less-populous species.

The most destructive force in the world is humanity and its burgeoning population. As the human population grows, more forested land must be cleared for agricultural use to produce needed food, which in turn causes less diversity of habitat, vegetation, and species. Development encourages more erosion, more contamination of water, and more pollution of the air. Also, when an area is paved, it prevents wildlife from living there. The burning of fossil fuels has definitely changed the weather of the world, causing more rain and flooding in some areas, while there is less rain and even drought in other areas. When there is melting of the polar ice cap, as has happened recently, it affects not only polar species, but all species throughout the world. (Photograph by Leonard Lee Rue III)

Bergmann's Law states that a larger body loses less heat per unit than does a smaller body. A larger body can also consume more food in order to build up a great layer of fat, which is needed to withstand the cold northern winters. Tropical deer, like this Florida Keys whitetail, don't need to lay by a store of body fat and thus do not need large bodies. (Photograph by Uschi Rue)

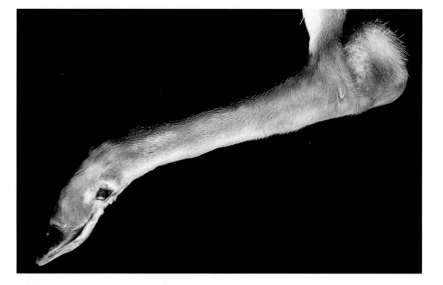

We humans walk upon our entire foot; hence we are plantigrade. All members of the *Cervidae* walk upon just their toenails, and are therefore unguligrade. This is the entire foot of a white-tailed deer. Its heel would be beneath the tarsal gland, on the right of the photo. (Photograph by Leonard Lee Rue III)

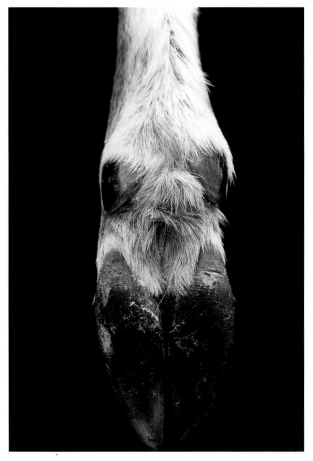

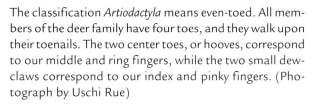

The classification *Artiodactyla* means even-toed. All members of the deer family have four toes, and they walk upon their toenails. The two center toes, or hooves, correspond to our middle and ring fingers, while the two small dewclaws correspond to our index and pinky fingers. (Photograph by Uschi Rue)

The caribou tracks in the mud show the imprint of the dewclaws as well as the two main hooves. Animals that live on tundra, or wet or swampy ground, such as caribou, reindeer, barasingha, marsh deer, Chinese water deer, and Peré David's deer have larger dewclaws, which give increased bearing surface to each foot. (Photograph by Uschi Rue)

Rub-urination occurs when deer—bucks, does, or fawns—rub their tarsal glands together as they urinate, so that the trickled urine carries the scent from the tarsal glands to the ground. This is a chemical means of communication. (Photograph by Leonard Lee Rue III)

Many species of *Cervidae*—including the fallow, axis, sika, pampas, musk, white-tailed, and mule deer, and the huemul, brocket, and elk—rub the bark from saplings and bushes and deposit their scent on the inner wood, creating both visual and chemical signposts. (Photograph by Leonard Lee Rue III)

Facing page: The whitened antlers tips on this bull elk are the result of his tearing up the turf with them to make wallows. This is also done by Thorold's deer, red deer, sambar, barasingha, Peré David's deer, huemuls, and moose. (Photograph by Uschi Rue)

Above: These young bull elk are only sparring, not actually fighting. Sparring is common among young males of any species that forms bachelor groups, including the white-tailed deer, elk, red deer, barasingha, caribou, and axis deer. Sparring is a constant striving for dominance. (Photograph by Uschi Rue)

Above: Mule deer, like all *Cervids*, have a matriarchal society. The bucks usually keep separate from the does and their fawns, except during rutting season. (Photograph by Uschi Rue)

Facing page: This barren-ground caribou bull's coat is getting its white cape and side stripe, which indicate that rutting season is about to begin. Elk, caribou, and moose have just one annual coat; they shed their heavy winter coat in late spring and their new coat grows longer all summer and fall. White-tailed, black-tailed, and mule deer have two coats of hair a year—a summer coat and a winter coat. (Photograph by Uschi Rue)

Albinism—a condition causing an animal to have an all white coat and pink eyes—may occur in any species. However, if there is any brown in the animal's coat, as with this white-tailed buck (below), it is known as a mutant. (Photographs by Leonard Lee Rue III)

Because of the tapetum at the back of all deer's eyes, a light shone at the deer will be reflected back as "eyeshine." This doubling of the light helps the deer see better in dark conditions. (Photograph by Bill Phillips)

Like many members of the deer family, mule deer are most active at dawn and dusk. (Photograph by Uschi Rue)

Access to water is vital to all deer species in any habitat around the world. This white-tailed buck is drinking at a small woodland stream. (Photograph by Len Rue Jr.)

Deer, regardless of the species, will feed in agricultural fields whenever they have the opportunity. These white-tailed deer are feeding in a farmer's clover hayfield. (Photograph by Uschi Rue)

Most members of the deer family benefit from the re-growth of vegetation that occurs after a forest fire or timber cutting. (Photograph by Uschi Rue)

A newborn white-tailed fawn is a "hider" species. Most deer species give birth to spotted fawns; the exceptions are the southern pudu, marsh and huemul deer, caribou, and moose. (Photograph by Leonard Lee Rue III)

The Moschidae Family

Common Names	Latin Names	Other Names
Musk Deer		
Himalayan	*Moschus chrysogaster*	Alpine Deer
Nepal	*Moschus leucogaster*	
Chinese	*Moschus fuscus*	
Forest	*Moschus berezovski*	Dwarf Deer
Siberian	*Moschus moschiferus*	

The Cervidae Family

Common Names	Latin Names	Other Names
Chinese Water Deer	*Hydropotes inermis*	
Tufted Deer	*Elaphodus cephalophus*	
Muntjacs		
Indian	*Muntiacus muntjak*	Barking Deer
Borneo	*Muntiacus atherodes*	Barking Deer
Reeve's	*Muntiacus reevesi*	Barking Deer
Fea's	*Muntiacus feae*	Barking Deer
Tibetan	*Muntiacus gongshanensis*	Barking Deer
Black	*Muntiacus crinifrons*	Barking Deer
Giant Muntjac	*Megamuntiacus vuquangensis*	
Fallow Deer	*Dama dama*	
Axis Deer		
Axis Deer	*Axis axis*	Chital Deer
Hog Deer	*Axis porcinos*	
Bawean or Kuhl's	*Axis kuhlii*	Java Sea Deer
Calamian	*Axis calamianensis*	Philippine Deer
Sambar		
Sambar	*Cervus unicolor*	
Suna Sambar, Rusa	*Cervus timorensis*	
Philippine Sambar	*Cervus mariannus*	
Visayan Sambar	*Cervus alfredi*	
Barasingha	*Cervus duvauceli*	Swamp Deer
Sika Deer	*Cervus nippon*	Japanese Deer
Thorold's Deer	*Cervus albirostris*	White-lipped Deer, Przewalski's Deer
Red Deer	*Cervus elaphus*	Maral
Wapiti/Elk (North America)	*Cervus canadensis*	
Peré David's Deer	*Elaphurus davidianus*	
Mule Deer	*Odocoileus hemionus*	Black-tailed Deer
White-tailed Deer	*Odocoileus virginianus*	
Marsh Deer	*Blastocerus dichotomus*	
Pampas Deer	*Ozotocerus bezoarticus*	Stinking Deer
Huemuls		
Peruvian	*Hippocamelus antisensis*	Guemel, Taruka
Chilean	*Hippocamelus bisulcus*	Guemel
Brocket Deer		
Red	*Mazama americana*	
Brown	*Mazama gouazoubira*	
Little Red	*Mazama rufina*	
Dwarf	*Mazama chunyi*	
Pudu		
Northern	*Pudu mephistophiles*	
Southern	*Pudu pudu*	
Moose	*Alces alces*	Elk
Caribou/Reindeer	*Rangifer tarandus*	
Roe Deer		
European	*Capreolus capreolus*	
Siberian	*Capreolus pygargus*	

Musk Deer

The musk deer, *Moschus*, is the species that causes the greatest disagreement between the taxonomists and biologists. Whereas it previously was classified as a family within the *Cervidae* family, most of the experts have recently re-assigned it to its own familial grouping, *Moschidae*.

Range: The musk deer is primarily a mountain animal that lives in forested areas. Its range stretches from Afghanistan in the west to Sakhalin Island in the east. It has a widespread range from the 65-degree latitude north in Siberia, south to Vietnam.

Description: There are five species of musk deer: Himalayan (*Moschus chrysogaster*), Nepal (*Moschus leucogaster*), Chinese (*Moschus fuscus*), forest (*Moschus berezovski*), and Siberian (*Moschus moschiferus*).

The five species vary in size, but are basically alike. They have an overall head and body length between 27 and 39 inches (700 and 1,000 mm). The tail length is short—0.7 to 2.34 inches (18 to 60 mm). The deer stand 19.5 to 31 inches (500 to 800 mm) high at the shoulder. They all have the exceptionally large haunches needed to propel them into instant flight, and they bound away from predators over the tops of vegetation. This mode of bounding is known as a saltatorial gait. The musk deer has a humped appearance because its hips are about 2 inches (50 mm) higher than its shoulders. The dewclaws are long and, by touching the ground, provide an extra grip when the musk deer stands on steep hillsides or rocks.

Its back and sides are covered with stiff, bristly hairs that are various shades of brown, while the belly hairs shade to gray. The musk deer that inhabit the densest forests have the darkest coats. They have white patches beneath the chin, on either side of the throat, and on the inner surfaces of the upper legs. At 5 inches (127 mm), the ears are fairly long for a forest animal.

Unlike other members of the deer family, musk deer have a gall bladder on the liver. They lack the typical preorbital and forehead scent glands and have no tarsal or metatarsal glands on their feet. Female musk deer have only two teats instead of the four that other members of the deer family have.

As a more primitive form of deer, musk deer have a unique feature in that the males do not have antlers; however, both male and female musk deer have downward, rear-curving canine teeth that are used in fighting. The male's teeth are about 2.95 inches (75 mm) in length, while those of the female are much shorter and do not protrude below her lips.

The musk deer gets its name from the musk-gland pouch located on the abdomen of the male, just in front of the penis sheath. This gland produces a brown, waxy musk that the deer uses in communication with its conspecifics. This musk is the most valuable animal product in the world, as it is used as a base for some of the most exotic and expensive perfumes. In 1999 the musk brought $45,000 for 35 ounces (1 kg) on the international market. Each adult male produces about 1 ounce (28 g) of musk each year, and it takes about thirty-six males to produce 35 ounces (1 kg) of musk. Thousands of these deer are shot so that the musk can be collected.

Habits: Musk deer are territorial, and will fight to defend a suitable area to ensure that the males, females, and young are able to meet food requirements. Such territories average about from 1 to 1.5 miles (1.6 to 2.4 km) across.

Lacking antlers, musk deer fight by slashing their opponents with their dagger-like canines. Consequently, they do not fight head-on, but stand shoulder-to-shoulder.

These deer lay out a network of trails. They frequently sleep in the same place each night, hollowing out beds in the duff of the forest floor. They are sedentary and do not move about much during daylight hours.

Musk deer feed on grasses, mosses, lichens, berry bushes, and the leaves and twigs of many forest plants. Because of the moisture in their forest environment, the vegetation is diverse, providing a wide array of forage. Like goats, musk deer are able to scramble up the inclined trunks of trees to feed above the ground. They often stand erect to reach the new, tender vegetation growing on the top of shrubs.

Musk deer are quite easily stressed by heat, but their heavy coats allow them to withstand the cold and snow that blankets their range during winter months.

Map of musk deer range in Asia

Communication: The musk gland reaches its peak production during rutting season, when a male deer heavily marks his territory to stimulate the female and to keep other males away from her. It is thought that this heavy marking also confuses predators, making it harder for them to locate the deer by scent.

As hiders, musk deer are seldom vocal, although when disturbed they do make a loud hissing noise much like a human sneeze. They have also been known to make a plaintive scream when injured.

Breeding: Rutting season occurs from mid-November to the end of December. Musk deer are basically monogamous, because food restrictions keep them confined to their home territories.

Birth and Young: The gestation period for musk deer is about 198 days. In some species, the female usually gives birth to a single fawn, while in other species twins are the norm. Fawns weigh a little over 1 pound (500 g) at birth and have spotted coats that help hide them from predators. The young grow rapidly and are weaned between three and four months of age. They are not sexually mature until about eighteen months. Captive musk deer in China have lived to be twenty years old.

Enemies: Because they are territorial and more or less solitary, musk deer are not exposed to as many parasites and pathogens as are herd animals. Musk deer are preyed upon by snow leopards and tigers.

Relationship with Humans: Unfortunately, habitat destruction and over-hunting of the deer for its valuable musk is causing a tremendous decline in its numbers. The annual kill reached as high as 500,000 animals a year in the 1990s, and it is estimated that the overall population has declined over 70 percent. Numerous attempts to raise the deer commercially for its musk have not proven feasible.

The Himalayan musk deer is one of the most primitive deer in the world. Instead of antlers, both males and females have canine tusks, which can be up to 2.95 inches (75 mm) in length. (Photograph © Heather Angel/Natural Visions)

Musk deer look like oversized rabbits. Like rabbits, they have strong hind legs that enable them to bound to safety when danger threatens. (Photograph © Gerald Cubitt)

The mottled pattern of this musk deer's coat helps the animal conceal in its sun-dappled forest habitat. (Photograph © Gerald Cubitt)

Chinese Water Deer

Range: The traditional range of water deer (*Hydropotes inermis*) is the entire Korean Peninsula and the adjoining northeastern portion of China.

Description: This stocky, short-legged little deer has a head and body length between 30 and 39 inches (775 and 1,000 mm) and a tail length of 2.3 to 2.9 inches (60 to 75 mm). It stands between 17.5 and 21 inches (450 and 550 mm) high at the shoulder and usually weighs between 24.2 and 30 pounds (11 and 14 kg).

Water deer are another primitive species of deer that does not have antlers. The male has little, rear-curving canine dagger teeth that measure about 2.5 inches (64 mm) in length. The female has much smaller curved canine teeth.

A water deer's coat is both thick and coarse. Its basic coloration is yellowish-brown with a white chin and throat. Hair on its back and sides has a peppering of fine black spots.

They have two scent glands in the groin area between the legs, as well as small preorbital glands. Water deer lack the tarsal and metatarsal glands found on most other deer.

Habits: As its name implies, this animal lives among the tall reeds and grasses along all types of streams, rivers, and lakes. It is a solitary animal, furtive and seldom seen. It is probably territorial because it is never found in herds. It is a strong swimmer, taking readily to the water to escape danger, to cross bodies of water, and to reach islands.

The water deer has a bounding gait it uses to dash back into cover when it feels threatened. Saltatorial bounding is physically demanding and cannot be kept up except for short periods of time. Because of this fact, the water deer does not venture far from the dense reeds and rushes in which it makes its home.

This deer's food consists primarily of reeds and rushes. It feeds upon many different grasses and emergent water plants, but probably gets more nutrition from the latter because the soil on riverbanks and lake bottoms contains more nutrients. Water deer often venture into cultivated fields and eat various vegetables and crops. Occasionally they will feed at the base of mountains.

Communication: Water deer give a harsh bark when they are disturbed or to warn other family members of impending danger. When angry or challenging a rival, males make what is described as a chittering noise, by rapidly clicking their teeth together.

Bucks mark vegetation in their areas with scent from their preorbital glands and use their inguinal glands for additional marking. They also mark by depositing their dung in heaps and adding to the heaps each time they pass by.

Breeding: Rutting season for water deer occurs in November and December. At such times, bucks fight by turning their necks and using their teeth to slash rivals. Their hides are thicker in the neck and shoulder areas to give them more protection.

Birth and Young: The gestation period for Chinese water deer is about 200 days. Does usually give birth to three fawns, but does have been known to have as many as five or six fetuses. No other deer in the world has such fecundity. Although the doe is capable of bearing so many young, it is not likely that she could raise more than three or four at one time.

Fawns are spotted and weigh a little over 2.2 pounds (1 kg). They mature rapidly; males reach sexual maturity at about six months of age, and females at eight months.

In captivity, one of these little deer lived to be thirteen years, eleven months old.

Enemies: The major predators of these deer are domestic and feral dogs. Because of the dearth of wildlife in the section of China and North Korea where water deer are found, there are few natural predators. The wolf and the tiger have been virtually exterminated there.

Relationship with Humans: Human development constantly encroaches upon the water deer's habitat. The deer is exterminated in some areas as a nuisance animal because it feeds readily upon commercially raised vegetables. This deer has been accorded status as a threatened species by the International Union for the Conservation of Nature (IUCN).

Male Chinese water deer can easily be told from the females because the males' canine tusks are much longer. (Photograph © Heather Angel/ Natural Visions)

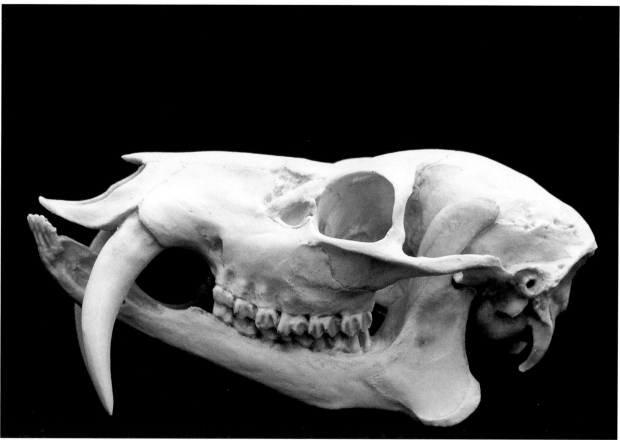

The curving canine teeth in this skull of a Chinese water deer measure 2.5 inches (63.5 mm) in length. (Photograph by Uschi Rue)

Tufted Deer

Range: The tufted deer (*Elaphdous cephalophus*) is found across southern China to eastern Tibet and northern Burma. It is a deer of the mountainous forest regions and is found at elevations between 984 and 14,760 feet (300 and 4,500 m).

Description: This slim-bodied deer has a head and body length of 42.9 to 62.4 inches (1,100 to 1,600 mm). Its tail is between 2.7 and 5.8 inches (70 and 150 mm) long. It stands between 19.5 and 27.3 inches (500 and 700 mm) high at the shoulder, and weighs between 37.4 and 110 pounds (17 and 50 kg).

The tufted deer gets its name from the little mane of stiff, bristly hairs that runs from the back of its skull down to its eyes. Its coat is exceptionally coarse and dark brown on the upper parts of the body. The underparts of the body and the undersurface of the tail are white; the head and neck are gray.

The tufted deer has antlers measuring less than 2 inches (50 mm) in length. The antlers are seldom seen because they are hidden in the long hair of the coat. This deer also has curved canine teeth that are a little over 1 inch (30 mm) in length. The tufted deer is midway in the evolutionary process between deer with long canine teeth and no antlers and deer with no canine teeth but well-developed antlers.

Habits: Although the tufted deer is a mountain creature, it does not stray far from water. It is solitary by nature, although it is often seen in pairs, as is common among deer that protect a territory. When discovered or flushed from the dense cover that it favors, the tufted deer bounds off with its tail held erect and bouncing from side to side, as white-tailed deer often do. Its tail provides a beacon for its young to follow in the gloom of night and in dark forests. The tufted deer feeds upon grasses, sprouts, leaves, twigs, and the buds of various forest plants.

Communication: When disturbed, the tufted deer gives a loud bark before it runs off. The bark warns its cohorts of danger and perhaps draws danger away from its young. This deer has large preorbital glands that it uses to mark its territory.

Breeding: Rutting season occurs in the months of November and December. At this time the male is particularly active ensuring a rival male does not attempt to breed with his mate.

Birth and Young: After a gestation period of about 210 days, the doe gives birth to a single fawn in May or June. Twins are a great rarity in this species. Being a singleton, the fawn is quite large, weighing between 3 and 4 pounds (1 to 2 kg). It has a spotted coat, which allows it to blend in with the sun-dappled forest floor, and thus escape detection. Fawns nurse for three to four months before being weaned. The young stay within parental territory until they are almost a year old. Maturity is reached at about eighteen months of age.

Tufted deer have been known to live to twelve years of age.

Enemies: The tufted deer is preyed upon by leopards, tigers, and bears. Jackals probably take some of the fawns.

Relationship with Humans: These deer are hunted extensively throughout their range. It is calculated that at least 100,000 out of an estimated population of 500,000 are trapped and shot each year for food.

In addition to the tuft of hair on top of its head, the tufted deer has two other outstanding characteristics: little antlers and long, curved canine teeth. (Photograph © Kenneth W. Fink/Photo Researchers)

Muntjacs

Range: There are seven species of muntjacs: Indian (*Muntiacus muntjak*), Borneo (*Muntiacus atherodes*), Reeve's (*Muntiacus reevesi*), Fea's (*Muntiacus feae*), Tibetan (*Muntiacus gongshanensis*), black (*Muntiacus crinifrons*), and giant (*Megamuntiacus vuquangensis*). Reeve's and black muntjacs are found in northern China; all others are found from Vietnam and India south through Indonesia. These deer may be found within their ranges at elevations from sea level up to 5,000 feet (1,525 m).

Description: Some taxonomists place the giant muntjac in its own genus of *Megamuntiacus*, but this classification is widely debated. George Schaller and E. S. Vrba have offered DNA evidence that the giant muntjac should be included in *Muntiacus*. This animal was unknown to science until 1994, when it was first described by Vietnamese biologist Do Tuoc. Subsequent investigators have shown that the giant muntjac is quite common in the mountains of northern Vietnam.

Muntjacs cannot be confused with any other deer because the males have the highest antler pedicles of any deer. With most deer the pedicle rises only 1 inch (25 mm) or so above the deer's frontal skull plate. The pedicle on a male muntjac averages about 6 inches (152 mm) in length. Where the males have long pedicles, females have small, bony knobs. At the base of each pedicle or knob is a bony ridge that extends down the skull, forming a raised V that extends to below the eyes. This ridge has given this deer the nickname "rib-face."

The Reeve's muntjac is the smallest species and the giant muntjac is the largest. The muntjacs have a head and body length of between 24.9 and 52.6 inches (640 and 1,350 mm) and a tail length of between 2.4 and 9.3 inches (65 and 240 mm). They have a shoulder height of 15.8 to 30.4 inches (406 to 780 mm), and weigh between 30.8 and 72.6 pounds (24 and 33 kg).

Only males have antlers, which grow out of long pedicles. These short antlers are between 2 and 4.18 inches (52 and 125 mm) in length and in most species are shed annually. Muntjacs in Borneo do not shed their antlers, which is unusual for even a tropical deer. On some muntjacs, the tips of the antlers have a definite backward hook, similar to those of a pronghorn antelope.

All muntjacs, including this Fea's, are also known as barking deer because of the dog-like barking sound they make when alarmed. (Photograph © Gerald Cubitt)

All muntjac males have short, stout canine teeth about 1 inch (25 mm) in length. Unlike other tusked deer, which have backward curving canines, those of muntjacs curve outward. They are still capable of inflicting slashing wounds. Muntjacs use their canines as offensive weapons and their antlers as defensive weapons. If males engage each other with their little antlers, it lessens the possibility of getting into a position to slash with their canines.

Muntjacs have short, soft hair on their bodies, with the ears being almost hairless. The coat varies in coloration from light tannish-yellow to deep brown. It is lighter in color on the belly and the insides of the legs.

Muntjacs have exceptionally large preorbital glands, which they flare widely when excited. They have small tarsal glands, but lack metatarsal glands.

Habits: Muntjacs are commonly called "barking deer." When surprised, or when they have discovered potential danger, these deer resound with a loud, staccato bark, which they often keep up for an hour or more. This barking can be heard for long distances. It serves the dual purpose of warning other muntjacs of potential danger and it lets a predator know it has been discovered, thus robbing the predator of the element of surprise needed to successfully catch prey.

The territorial behavior of muntjacs varies with

the species, and even within a species, according to the type of habitat each inhabits. Those that live in heavily forested areas will maintain a territory, whereas those who live on the edge of a forest and feed more in open areas do not. Muntjacs are not found in large herds, but they are much more sociable when living in open areas. As might be expected, the more social males engage in more sparring for dominance than do the more solitary, forest-dwelling males. (This pattern of behavior is common to all members of the deer family.)

Muntjacs lay out a network of trails to facilitate easy movement through heavy cover. Like many members of the deer family, muntjacs are more active in the early morning and late afternoon, and remain bedded the rest of the day. They feed upon a great many types of vegetation, eating grasses, forbs, woody browse, leaves, berries, and fallen fruit.

Communication: In addition to the loud barking already discussed, muntjacs engage in olfactory communication. The flaring of their preorbital glands releases scent molecules into the air. By rubbing those opened glands against vegetation, they liberally paint their personal odors all around. Muntjacs also make dung heaps and urine markings. Like white-tailed deer, they also do rub-urination, by trickling urine over their tarsal glands. The urine adheres to the lipids extruded from the tarsal glands, turning the glands black in color.

Breeding: The more northern forms of muntjacs usually breed during December and January, and the females give birth in June or July. More tropical muntjacs have no set breeding period, with breeding and births occurring any time of the year.

Birth and Young: Little is known about the actual gestation period, but muntjacs have a postpartum estrus and can be bred within a week after giving birth. It has been documented that about 243 days elapse between birthings. Some researchers believe that the gestation period might be as short as 210 to 220 days. Usually a single, spotted fawn is born. They mature rapidly and are breeding before they are a year old.

In captivity a Reeve's muntjac lived to be nineteen years, eight months old.

Enemies: Domestic and feral dogs kill some muntjacs, as do leopards and tigers. There are records of some muntjacs being taken by giant pythons that inhabit the same range.

Relationship with Humans: Habitat destruction is the main reason for the decline in muntjac numbers, but they are also heavily hunted in regions where people are hungry for protein.

Because of their elongated pedicles, muntjacs cannot be confused with any other deer in the world. (Photograph © Erwin & Peggy Bauer)

Female muntjacs lack the long pedicles that show so prominently on the males. (Photograph © Gerald Cubitt)

Fallow Deer

Range: The original range of the fallow deer (*Dama dama*) was around the eastern end of the Mediterranean Sea, southern Europe, Turkey, the island of Rhodes, and as far east as Iran; the deer are still found in these areas today. Fallow deer were a favorite animal in early game and deer parks. They were imported into every country in Europe, and are still found in many town parks throughout Europe. Over the years, many fallow deer escaped from the parks, and wild herds have become established in most European countries on forest preserves. This deer has been widely imported into North and South America, Asia, Australia, and New Zealand. It is probably the best known of all deer species.

Description: The fallow deer has a head and body length of 50.7 to 68.2 inches (1,300 to 1,750 mm). Its tail is 5.8 to 8.9 inches (150 to 230 mm) long. The deer stands 31.2 to 40.9 inches (792 to 1,039 mm) at the shoulder. It has a stocky body and weighs between 88 and 220 pounds (40 and 100 kg).

The adult bucks' antlers are widely palmated and may measure 24.7 to 36.6 inches (635 to 940 mm) along the main beam from the pedicle to the tip. They have an inside spread of 11.8 to 29.7 inches (305 to 762 mm). The antlers are usually carried until April, and the new set starts to grow immediately, becoming fully grown by September.

The fallow deer has more color variations than any other deer in the world. Its basic summer color is a rich russet red with two rows of white spots running down its back and hundreds of white spots covering its body. There is a white horizontal stripe just above its belly. The Persian subspecies has a deeper brown basic coloration; the winter coat of this color phase is grayish-brown with barely detectable spots.

In addition to the basic colors, fallow deer sometimes have a smoky blue-gray coat and some are jet black. The deer with the jet black coats have dark brown spots instead of white. There are white fallow

Like the axis deer of Asia, fallow deer have a spotted coat all their life. (Photograph by Leonard Lee Rue III)

This melanistic fallow buck has such a dark coat that his spots are almost impossible to see. (Photograph by Leonard Lee Rue III)

deer that have normal colored eyes, and there are albino fallow deer that have pink eyes.

A conspicuous feature of all fallow bucks is the large, prominent "Adam's apple" situated about 6 inches (152 mm) beneath the jaw. This enlargement of the buck's larynx is a resonatory chamber and allows the buck to make a deep, roaring grunt sound. They have a pronounced preorbital gland, and they also have preputial glands located above the long hair tufts on the tip of the penis sheath. These hair tufts retain urine.

Fallow deer lack the canine teeth of more primitive deer species.

Habits: The fallow deer is primarily a grazing species, feeding mainly upon a great variety of grasses and forbs. However, it must have wooded areas to which it can escape when pursued by predators. In such areas, it feeds upon browse. As with most deer, fallow deer feed most actively from dawn until two hours after sunrise, and again from late afternoon until dark. After feeding in the open fields, the deer retire to a secluded bedding area in the forest to chew their cud.

In different areas, the deer vary from being social and found in herds of up to thirty animals to the males being quite solitary.

In moving from one area to another, fallow deer walk, trot, and, if pursued, bound or gallop. On hilly terrain, fallow deer often stot like mule deer. From personal observation, I would say that fallow deer are not as alert as white-tailed deer, nor can they run as fast or jump as high.

The females of most *Cervidae* species are smaller than the males. Note the difference in body size between this fallow doe and the three bucks. (Photograph by Leonard Lee Rue III)

Communication: Male fallow deer make visual signposts by rubbing slender saplings and brush with their antlers, exposing the white inner bark. They then individualize these rubbings with scent from their pre-orbital glands. When excited, both sexes open these glands so that the scent can be carried by the air currents.

Just as the elk (wapiti) self-advertises by urinating on his long neck hair and the moose by soaking his "bell" in a urine-soaked wallow, the fallow buck urinates frequently on the hair of his penis sheath. The female fallow deer has long hairs at the end of her tail that she saturates with urine by not raising her tail. This is a common practice and not done just during the rutting season.

The enlarged larynx of the buck allows him to make a low-pitched, rolling grunting sound during rutting season. Fallow deer are very vocal. They are probably exceeded in vocalizations only by elk bugling and red deer roaring.

In courting the female, the male turns his antlers from side to side, so that they are more visible to the female as he approaches. This antler-turning is usually accompanied by a loud roaring.

Breeding: North of the equator, rutting season occurs in October and November, and south of the equator it occurs in April and May. During rutting season, males fight viciously to defend a territory. In grassy open areas, fallow bucks establish a lek territory, much as the Kob antelope of Africa do. The lek is usually located on a small hilltop with the choicest territory being the apex of the hill. Each buck has a piece of territory that may be no more than 200 feet (61 m) across. The biggest, strongest buck will be in possession of the most desirable piece of territory at the apex.

Females' estrus cycles are closely synchronized so that most of them will need to be bred at the same time. Most females prefer to be bred by the dominant male and will seek him out at the top of the hill. As a female crosses a male's territory, the male will run and prance toward the female, trying to entice her to stay in his territory. As she is about to leave one male's territory, the next male will dash to the border and often clashes with the male whose territory she is leaving. Even the most dominant male can only hold the apex for a few days and then will have to leave it to get water. After drinking, he will then have to fight his way back up to the apex, which is claimed by the second-most-powerful buck as soon as the first buck vacates the area.

The prancing, patrolling, fighting, and breeding take their toll on the bucks, which can lose 20 percent or more of their body weight in a period of several weeks. So it is a good thing that rutting season is short.

Birth and Young: The gestation period for fallow deer is between 225 and 230 days. The female usually gives birth to a single spotted fawn; twins are a rarity. Fawns average about 6 pounds (3 kg) in weight. Their spotted coat provides them with excellent camouflage. They are hiders and are visited by their mother three to five times in a twenty-four-hour period so they can nurse.

Some females are capable of being bred when they are six to seven months old, but males are not mature enough to breed until they are sixteen to eighteen months old. Even though males are then capable of breeding, young males are usually bypassed by females in favor of older, mature bucks.

In captivity fallow deer have been known to live to twenty years of age.

Enemies: Domestic and feral dogs are the major predators in Europe. Lions and leopards prey on deer in South Africa, and dingos take deer in Australia.

Relationship with Humans: It is humans who extirpated the fallow deer from much of its original range, and it is humans that have introduced and protected the deer in its present locations. Fallow deer are widely hunted where feral herds exist and on the many hunting preserves maintained for just that purpose.

The extreme palmation of this fallow buck's antlers makes it a real trophy. (Photograph by Leonard Lee Rue III)

Axis Deer

Range: The axis or chital deer (*Axis axis*) is found primarily in the lowlands of the Indian Peninsula and Nepal. The axis hog deer (*Axis porcinos*) has a much wider range, and is found from Pakistan to India, Burma, and Thailand. The Bawean and Calamian axis deer (*Axis kuhlii* and *Axis calamianesis*) live only in the Philippines and on the two islands off Java for which they are named.

Description: Axis deer are probably the most vividly marked of all deer. The permanent white spots on their coats appear whiter and the russet-red hair color brighter than that of even fallow deer. Axis deer have large white bibs, or throat patches; white bellies; and light colored legs. The color varies by species and by season. Hog deer, for instance, have darker coats and indistinct spotting.

Axis deer have a head and body length of 42.9 to 68.25 inches (1,100 to 1,750 mm). They have a rather long tail, measuring from 4.9 to 14.8 inches (128 to 380 mm). Adult males stand 23.4 to 39 inches (594 to 990 mm) high at the shoulder, and weigh between 60 and 242 pounds (27 and 110 kg). Chital deer are slender, graceful deer, while the other three *Axis* species have shorter legs and blockier bodies. The latter three deer are collectively called hog deer because, instead of bounding away over the underbrush when frightened, they run and plow through the dense vegetation as a hog would do. The habits of all three species of hog deer are basically the same.

Axis deer are referred to as three-tined deer because of their unique antlers. The main beam sweeps back, then forward, and has just one backward pointing tine. The brow tines project forward from the base of the main beam at about 90 degrees and bend up at the tips. The main beam of the Indian chital deer averages between 30 and 38 inches (760 and 960 mm) in length. The main beams on the three hog deer spe-

The hog deer is a stocky-bodied little deer that inhabits the dense forest areas of southeastern Asia. (Photograph by Leonard Lee Rue III)

Map of axis deer range in India

The axis or chital deer are found in the lowlands of both India and Nepal. (Photograph by Leonard Lee Rue III)

cies are between 15.5 and 24 inches (390 and 609 mm). On rare occasions, these deer will have an additional rear-pointing tine on each main beam. Hog deer have elongated hair-covered pedicles, although they are not as long as those of muntjacs.

As they are tropical deer, there is no precise time for the production or casting of antlers. Even deer living in the same area may have antlers in different stages of development.

Chital deer rarely have even rudimentary canine teeth. Young hog deer do, but lose them as they become adults; the cavity left by the lost tooth fills up with bone.

The coat of all four species is coarse, almost bristly, and quite long on the animal's flanks. Even seasonal color changes are not tied to a particular season because of the influence of the tropics. These deer do not get a winter coat.

Habits: The chital deer of India and Nepal are primarily grazing animals and, as such, are much more sociable than are the three hog deer. Chital deer are found on grasslands bordered by woodland, into which they escape if molested. Grazing by domestic cattle benefits chital deer because cattle eat the coarser, larger grasses while the deer eat the new replacement shoots. Grasses, forbs, farm crops, some browse, fallen forest fruits, and flowers make up the chital deer's diet.

Hog deer are more often solitary, and inhabit woodlands, jungles, and areas of more dense riverside vegetation. They feed upon grasses, forbs, and fallen fruit, but shoots, buds, and tiny twigs of various types of browse form a good part of their diet.

Like most deer, both of these species are most active in the early morning and late afternoon. These deer can be easily stressed by the heat of the day, so they move little in the middle of the day. If the heat is frequent, these deer often become completely nocturnal.

Whereas chital deer tend to run off as a herd when disturbed, hog deer run off separately, each seeking its own trail. The female hog deer is likely to raise her tail, exposing the white undersurface, so that her fawn can follow her. Both chital and hog deer take readily to water to swim to safety, an action especially important to the hog deer, which can readily be run down by a big dog on land because of its shortened legs.

When chital deer feed as a group, in herds of up to one hundred animals, the males usually feed in the center, surrounded by the females and their young. Young males make up the outer edge of the herd. This pattern is directly opposite to the way white-tailed deer feed. With whitetails, males are usually on the outer periphery of the group.

Communication: Chital deer are vocal, while hog deer are less vocal. During rutting season, male chital deer give out coarse bellows and throaty but high-pitched growls. Females bark when alarmed and also when herded by males during rutting season.

Both males and females have large preorbital glands that can be everted, allowing the scent to be dispersed by air currents. These glands are also used to deposit an individualized scent on vegetation. Chital deer also engage in a practice called "preaching," in which a male stands erect on his hind legs and marks overhead branches with scent from his preorbital glands.

Both chital and hog deer make rubs with their antlers, taking off the dark outer bark of a tree, thus exposing the white inner bark and making a visible signpost. Wooded areas next to the grasslands where herds of chital feed have the bark rubbed off almost every sapling and tree as far as the eye can see. In some instances the rubbings are so complete that the saplings and trees are girdled and die, thus preventing their encroachment on the grasslands that these deer favor.

Chital males self-advertise by dripping urine down the long hairs hanging below the penis sheath. They also drip urine in scrapes, which they make by pawing the soil with their front feet. All four species of axis deer leave scent on the ground from their interdigital glands.

Tendons slipping off the bones of the chital deer's toes produce a cracking sound similar to that made by a herd of migrating caribou (reindeer). It is thought that this sound helps the deer keep in touch with each other at night when they are not vocalizing. It tells them when one of their own is approaching in the darkness.

Breeding: axis deer, which are basically tropical, have no hard and fast breeding season. Just as the male's antler development is relegated to no particular season, the female's estrus may occur in any month of the year. Only males that have hardened, peeled antlers can be dominant bucks. Thus, dominance is on a rotation plan; once their antlers are cast or new ones are growing, the previously dominant males become subordinate as other bucks cycle into dominance.

Dominant bucks display for the other bucks and the does by carrying their heads high, everting their preorbital glands, raising their tail, approaching other deer in a sidling fashion, and hissing.

Sparring is common among the hard-antlered chital males. Hog deer do less sparring, but are extremely aggressive and do much more fighting. It is this aggressive nature that makes it so hard to keep hog deer in captivity. There are many accounts of hog deer attacking their keepers and even attacking much larger males of different species. This situation is most unusual because most small animals simply will not attack a larger one.

Fighting is uncommon among chital bucks. One thing I noticed when I photographed chital deer in Nepal was that, while the bucks were in velvet, they were not very wary. When they felt in danger, they retreated from the grasslands to the edge of the woodlands, and stood and watched with an alert head held in a high position. Once the velvet had been peeled from their antlers, the bucks were exceptionally wary, and they did not come into the grassland in the daylight.

Chital bucks make no attempt to corral into a personal harem any females from the big herd. As each female comes into estrus, she is sought out by a dominant buck, who then just tries to breed the doe while keeping lesser bucks at bay. The buck approaches the doe with his head in a low, outstretched neck position. The doe will frequently make short runs, with the buck in hot pursuit. When she is ready to stand, he will court her by caressing her body and her vulva. This courtship is almost identical to that of white-tailed deer.

All axis deer, like this buck, retain their spotted coats all their life. (Photograph by Leonard Lee Rue III)

Birth and Young: Both chital and hog deer have a rather long gestation period, considering their size. Young are born 225 to 230 days after breeding. There is usually just one fawn, although on occasion there may be twins. Fawns are spotted at birth and are hiders, but most follow after their mother in just about a week's time. The mother nurses her young only three to four times in a twenty-four-hour period.

The young grow rapidly and most young females breed before they are one year old. Older does may breed only eighteen days after giving birth, so that they will be bred twice during some years. Because of this fact, the recruitment rate for these deer is high.

In captivity, axis deer have been known to live for over twenty years.

Enemies: The two most important enemies of chital and hog deer are tigers, and wild dogs called dholes. Dholes hunt in packs. The deer either run before the dogs are close or will sometimes attack by using their antlers or striking with their forefeet. The deer have little defense against tigers except by running, so they are extremely alert to all warning cries from birds and monkeys that mark the passage of a tiger. The deer try to keep enough distance between themselves and the tiger to make a stalk impractical. All species of axis deer are also preyed upon occasionally by large pythons that live in the area.

Relationship with Humans: Chital deer have, of late, adopted another trick to foil their predators. Because both dholes and tigers try to minimize their encounters with humans, the chital deer have learned to retreat to the edges of villages for safety. At night they will even enter the villages and mingle with the villagers' cattle.

The burgeoning human population in India and other Southeast Asian countries constantly requires that more land be made available for agriculture. It is habitat destruction that poses the greatest threat to both chital and hog deer.

Because of its antler formation, this axis buck belongs to a group of Asiatic deer known as three-antlered deer. They have just three tines on each side of their head. (Photograph by Len Rue Jr.)

Sambar

Range: The four species of sambar deer (*Cervus unicolor*, *Cervus timorensis*, *Cervus mariannus*, and *Cervus alfredi*) have a wide range that includes India, Bangladesh, Sri Lanka, Malaysia, Indonesia, and the Philippines. Sambar deer have been introduced to New Zealand and Australia and can be found on some game ranches in the United States.

Description: The western subspecies of this deer are the largest, while those of the Philippines are the smallest. They range in head and body length from 39 to 96 inches (1,000 to 2,460 mm). The tail length is 3.1 to 9.75 inches (80 to 250 mm). Sambar stand from 21.4 to 62.4 inches (550 to 1,600 mm) high at the shoulder, and weigh between 88 and 570 pounds (40 and 260 kg).

Sambar are typical three-tined deer. The main antler beam can measure up to 39 inches (1,000 mm) in length. The brow tine is the largest tine and projects forward at right angles to the main beam. The second set of tines also project forward, but at a much less severe angle. The tips of the main beam constitute the third set of tines. There is no set season for sambar to produce or cast antlers, since they are basically tropical animals. In any month of the year, stags may be found without antlers, with antlers in velvet, or with hardened antlers. In Malaysia, some stags have been known to carry their antlers for two years without shedding. The record length of a sambar stag's antlers is 50.1 inches (1,276 mm).

In coloration, most sambar are various shades of brown or brownish-gray, with dark brown the most common color. Their hair is coarse, and some large adult males have manes of darker hair. There is usually a white throat patch, a white belly, a white underside to the tail, and some shades of white on the inside of the animal's legs. Sambar may raise their tails to display the white underside, but the hairs of the tail cannot be flared. The raised tail also allows the white rump hairs to be seen.

Sambar's ears are rather large and well rounded. These deer have large preorbital glands that are widely everted when the sambar is alerted or when one stag challenges another. The preorbital glands figure prominently in the marking of vegetation. Sambar deer have a large, hairless glandular area in the middle of their throat patch, and also have small metatarsal glands.

Both sexes of sambar deer have rudimentary maxillary canine teeth.

Habits: As to be expected of an animal that has such a wide range, the sambar is highly adaptable. It is found from the ocean's edge to sub-alpine mountains at elevations up to 8,800 feet (2,700 m). Although it feeds upon a wide variety of coarse grasses, it has a comparatively narrow muzzle, which is indicative of a selective feeder with a diet made up largely of browse. The choice of grazing or browsing mainly depends upon whether the sambar is living in a heavily forested area or along the edge of meadows. Sambar are frequently found feeding in the shallow water of lakes and ponds. Sambar stags have also been found eating seaweed and kelp at the edge of the ocean.

No matter where it lives, the sambar will retreat to forested areas to seek shade during the heat of the day. Like moose, sambar deer often seek relief from the heat by standing in water.

The sambar may be solitary or gregarious, again depending upon the type of terrain it inhabits. In forested areas, does live together in family groups, while older stags are either strictly loners or associate only with one or two other males. Where the habitat is more open, sambar are often found in herds numbering as many as fifty individuals, but even then males tend to keep to the periphery of the herd.

Because they are large animals, sambar are one of the few members of the deer family that will put up an aggressive defense against the dholes that hunt them. They also don't hesitate to attack domestic dogs that harass them. Native hunters often take advantage of this trait and use dogs to force sambar to stand until they can get close enough to kill them. Like many members of the deer family, sambar will take to water to escape predators. With their long legs, sambar have solid footing in water that is deep enough to force a predator to swim.

Although the sambar frequents wet areas, it has the small hooves needed to run fast on hard ground. It is a well-muscled animal that can run at speeds of 35 miles per hour (56 kph). It is a saltatorial runner and easily jumps over low bushes and shrubs to put a

Facing page: Like the axis deer, the sambar is also classified as a three-antlered deer. The sambar is a large-bodied deer that has a large range extending from coastal regions to high mountains. (Photographs by Leonard Lee Rue III)

screen between itself and its pursuer. And like most deer, the sambar knows that its best defense may be to just stand absolutely motionless in heavy cover and let the danger walk on by.

Communication: Sambar utilize all five senses and many types of communication, often two or three different types all at the same time.

As mentioned, the sambar has large preorbital glands that it can flare widely, releasing scent molecules into the air when the deer is angry, threatening, frightened, or being threatened. When facing either a rival stag or predators such as dholes and dogs, the sambar flares its long, coarse mane, lays its ears back, flares its preorbital glands, and hisses loudly. It may also stamp its feet, sending vibrations through the earth and sound through the air.

The sambar probably stands erect more easily and more often than most other deer, and it uses this ability to feed upon high foliage. Stags also stand erect to hook the overhead branches with their antlers and to deposit scent on the high branches from their preorbital glands, a practice called "preaching."

Long, coarse neck hair on the sanbar indicates that it engages in self-advertisement, as do many other members of the *Cervus* family. Like the elk, the sambar stag urinates on his neck frequently, but unlike the elk, he does not spray the urine between his front legs. Instead the sambar extends his penis sideways, turns his head to the same side, and then saturates his head and neck with urine. The strong smell of urine is a threat to rival males and a stimulant to females.

Sambar stags also frequently make wallows. Using their antler tips, they plow the ground, tearing up and turning chunks of sod or, in damp areas, gobs of mud. The white tips on their brown antlers bear mute testimony to this activity. The stag then paws the earth with his forefeet and urinates in the freshly turned earth. Then, lying down in the saturated soil, the stag rolls about in the wallow, coating his long neck hair with the odorous mud. He deposits the mud and urine on trees by rubbing them with his neck. Stags also grate their antlers against bushes, saplings, and trees, exposing the light inner bark and depositing their scent thereon.

Breeding: Sambar stags are territorial and gather together a harem of six to eight hinds and their young. They do not chase after the hinds, but attract females with their scent and their roaring bellows. The hinds are attracted to the largest males. Even at a distance, they know the size of a male because the larger the male, the deeper his voice. During rutting season, a stag's constant roaring is a challenge to any potential rival and a promised threat to stags willing to accept the challenge. As a tropical species, sambar may breed at any time of the year, but most breeding activity takes place from September through January.

Only equal animals fight and if neither stag gives way to the overt threat of the other's body language and odor, it becomes a case of "put up or shut up." The stags approach each other with a sidling gait, their manes raised, their preorbital glands everted, their ears laid back, and their heads turned slightly away. They walk stiff-legged and hiss loudly like a leaky steam valve. Then, suddenly, like a pair of rams, they will rise fully erect, run forward a few steps, and crash head on into their opponent.

Fights are of short duration, seldom lasting more than a minute or so. The stags fight with legs spread wide, each stag trying to push his opponent off his feet. It takes but a few moments for both stags to know which is the stronger, and it is then up to the lesser stag to break free and dash off without being gored. Even so, the winner is often able to inflict a puncture wound in the lower hind quarters as his opponent departs. Having proven he is superior, there is little need for a long chase; the winning stag seldom pursues the vanquished one.

The sambar stag, while keeping his harem together and other males away, actively courts the estrus hind during the twenty-four or so hours that she is actually receptive. The stag caresses her head, body, and vulva with his tongue. He lays his head across her body. Females often act coy and rebuff a stag's advances by turning away sharply so they stand head to tail to each other. Eventually the stag's body contact and odor will stimulate the female so that she will stand.

Birth and Young: The gestation period for sambar is about 235 to 240 days, with most young born between May and July, although with the tropical subspecies, births occur at any time of the year. Hinds usually have just a single calf that will weigh about 22 pounds (10 kg). Calves have spotted coats and remain well hidden for the first two to three weeks of life, then follow after their dams. The young stay with the female for at least a year.

Enemies: The dholes, hunting in packs, are probably sambar deer's most frequently encountered predator. Domestic dogs, leopards, tigers, and the occasional python also prey upon sambar.

Relationship with Humans: The sambar, because of its huge size, is an important game species wherever it is found. As usual, humans' constant encroachment on sambar habitat is the reason for its steady decline throughout its entire range. The constant civil strife and wars that have occurred throughout much of the sambar's range over the past fifty years have brought a tremendous influx of guns into the area, and a breakdown of laws makes it almost impossible to protect the animals.

Barasingha

Range: The three subspecies of barasingha (*Cervus duvalucelii*), or swamp deer, are found only in central and northern India and southwestern Nepal.

Description: An adult male barasingha stands 44 to 46 inches (1,117 to 1,168 mm) high at the shoulder, measures about 71 inches (1,800 mm) in head and body length, and has a tail length of 4.6 to 7.8 inches (120 to 200 mm). Stags weigh an average of 506 to 622 pounds (230 to 283 kg). Hinds weigh between 305 and 320 pounds (138 and 145 kg).

Barasingha have two annual coats. Their summer coat is a bright reddish-brown, with side and belly hair slightly lighter in coloration. The throat, chin, inner legs, and underside of the tail are white. These animals have white spots running down either side of the spine and scattered along the sides. The spots are very noticeable on the summer coat, but much less so

when the animals are in their dark-gray winter coats. Adult stags grow long, dark neck hairs in their winter coat.

Young males grow a set of pedicles before they are six months old, and a set of spike antlers when they are one and a half years old. At age two and a half, stags grow a rack of antlers that have long brow tines projecting forward at about a 90 degree angle from the main beam. The antlers sweep back and then forward with a number of tines projecting from the top of the main beam. In the Hindu language, the name *barasingha* means "twelve tines," and these deer often have six tines on each main beam, making twelve tines total. The biggest, oldest stags sometimes have fourteen tines total. The record length for a main beam is 41 inches (1,041 mm). Barasingha's antlers are smooth except for the lateral blood lines and do not have the rough perlation so commonly found on the antlers of other members of the deer family, such as the roe buck and the white-tailed deer.

In central India, barasingha's antlers are usually cast in May and June and new growth starts shortly thereafter. In northern India and Nepal, antlers are usually cast in March, and thus new antler growth is two months ahead of these deer's southern counterparts. (Similarly, in the United States, deer living above the 33-degree latitude cast their antlers before those living below this parallel.)

Barasingha have preorbital, tarsal, and metatarsal glands. I can find no record of these deer having maxillary canine teeth.

Habits: Barasingha are almost exclusively grazing animals, which designates them as animals that will be found primarily in open grassland since very little grass grows in forests. Although these animals are conditioned to being out in the open most of the time, barasingha do go into forest areas, primarily to seek shade during the heat of the day. Whenever possible, barasingha prefer to be in swampy, marshy, or riverine areas. They not only feed in these areas, but also seek refuge in water to escape the heat and predators. They are strong swimmers and their long, wide hooves prevent them from sinking in mud. Because they live where the ground is soft and has no stones, barasingha's hooves are not worn down as they would

The barasingha is a marsh-dwelling animal that is preyed heavily upon by tigers in India. (Photograph © Erwin & Peggy Bauer)

be on hard ground. However, barasingha in central India do live on drier, slightly hilly ground and they still have larger hooves than other deer of similar size and weight.

As open-area animals, barasingha are social and are found in large herds, with some herds numbering up to 500 individuals. As herd animals, they have a social structure with a dominance ranking, but they exhibit less aggression than most herd animals. Also, unlike most deer that herd, barasingha stags are mixed throughout the herd instead of relegated to the periphery.

A surprising fact is that barasingha often eat coarse dried grasses, even when fresh green shoots can be found. Most grazers prefer new shoots, because they are more palatable and because emergent vegetation is always higher in nutrition.

Barasingha may be found grazing at any hour of the day, but they are most active in the two to three hours after daybreak and the two to three hours before darkness falls. They apparently do not move about or feed much at night; they can usually be found in the early morning very close to where they were last seen at dark.

When barasingha are disturbed, they may either run off at a gallop of about 35 miles per hour (56 kmh)

or they may stot. Stotting is usually kept up for no more than ten to twelve jumps as it is very tiring. Most deer that stot live in mountainous country; barasingha avoid even low hills, which indicates that their stotting is a holdover from an earlier evolutionary time.

Communication: Deer that live in forested areas use little vocalization because the sound is absorbed by the trees; deer like the barasingha that inhabit wide, open areas are much more vocal. As they live in large groups or herds, vocalizations are important, particularly to warn of danger. Barasingha have a high-pitched bark or yelp that they give as soon as danger is spotted. It's a call that is taken up by other members of the herd and puts them all on the highest alert. The barking is often kept up for twenty minutes or more, or until they are satisfied that the threat has passed.

During rutting season, stags do a lot of deep tonal bellowing, both to attract females and to challenge rivals. Stags do not often hook bushes with their antlers, but they do use their antlers to tear up turf to make wallows. They urinate in the muddy wallows and then lie down in the mud, adding the scent from their tarsal and metatarsal glands to the mixture. After they have coated themselves with mud, they often transfer the mud and their scent to trees, by rubbing on them. Stags also rub their preorbital glands on vegetation and brush and urinate on their long neck hairs in self-advertisement.

The hind has a high-pitched yelp she uses to locate her calf and the calf responds with a high MAAA!

Both stags and hinds employ a lot of body language, and the one most commonly seen is the sign of dominance. The dominant animal points its muzzle straight up to the sky, displaying its white throat patch and stretching its neck as high as it will go. The higher the head is held, the higher the rank of dominance.

Breeding: Breeding season is a prolonged affair, as females' estrus periods are not synchronized. This is probably just as well because the females are monoestrus—they do not recycle every month as many other species of deer do—and each must be bred within her single, short, yearly estrus period. Rutting season appears to extend from October to February, with a peak in December and January for central India, and a peak in November in northern India and Nepal.

At peak time, each adult stag tries to maintain a harem of as many females as he can control. Harems of up to thirty hinds have been reported. Although barasingha stags do a lot of formalized sparring, actual fighting is rare.

In courtship, the stag usually approaches from a distance with his head held high. When he gets close to the hind, he drops his head, extends his neck, and runs to her in a crouching position. He will sniff her vulva to check for the pheromones that denote estrus. If she is in heat, he will nuzzle her and stay by her side until he breeds her.

Although dominant stags gather harems, they do not attempt to drive every other male out of the area, as other species such as elk (wapiti) do. Instead, they just seclude a single estrus female to keep other stags from breeding her. Thus stags expend much less energy and come through rutting season in much better shape than do emaciated elk bulls.

Birth and Young: The gestation period for barasingha is approximately 240 to 250 days, with actual timing determined by the nutrition in the food that is available to the hind. Most calves are born during or after the rainy season, when there is food in abundance for the lactating female. Prior to giving birth, pregnant females leave the herd and retire to some brushy area, which provides suitable cover to screen both the female and her newborn calf from view. At this time, hinds become exceptionally wary.

Barasingha hinds usually give birth to singletons; twins are a great rarity. Calves weigh between 20 and 25 pounds (9 and 11 kg) at birth and have the spotted coat of a "hider" species. Hinds stay in the general area in which their calves are hiding, but they do not stay in the immediate vicinity. By so doing, hinds may be able to lure danger away from their hiding young, and they avoid leaving their body odor near the calf since the odor might attract danger to the calf. Because calves remain almost motionless and because hinds consume the calves' feces and urine that was voided while they nursed, calves have practically no betraying odor.

In two to three weeks' time, calves follow after their mothers, who then rejoin the herd. A calf's spotted coat is lost at about six weeks of age. The young grow rapidly, but are not sexually mature enough to breed until they are sixteen months or older.

In captivity, a barasingha has lived to twenty-three years old.

Enemies: The tiger is the main predator of barasingha, and it is the one most frequently encountered, as both animals favor the wet areas. Pythons take calves when the opportunity presents itself.

Perhaps the greatest threat to barasingha is the spread of disease, such as brucellosis, from domestic cattle. At times, entire herds of barasingha have succumbed to such cattle diseases. At other times, the deer's immune system has been so weakened by such exposure that natural mortality becomes high. George Schaller found the annual recruitment rate in some areas to be only 7 percent, which denotes a species in sharp decline.

Relationship with Humans: The barasingha population has declined so steadily that it has been placed on the IUCN's endangered species list. A lot of the barasingha's wet, marshland habitat has been taken over by farmers and converted into rice fields. Poaching is a constant threat, as are cattle diseases and predation. The barasingha faces so many threats that it is feared it will soon become extinct.

Wild herds of Asiatic sika deer were imported into and have become established in the United States. (Photograph by Leonard Lee Rue III)

Sika Deer

Range: Sika deer are found in southeastern Siberia, Korea, most of China, the Tibetan plateau, northern Vietnam, Japan, and Taiwan. They are often referred to as the Japanese deer because of their Latin name, *Cervus nippon*, and also because *sika* means *deer* in Japanese. There are wild sika deer herds established in the United States, with huntable populations in Maryland. There are also many wild herds established throughout Europe and England.

Description: Sika deer are chunky-bodied deer. They measure 37 to 54 inches (950 to 1,400 mm) in head and body length and have a tail length between 2.9 and 5 inches (75 and 130 mm). They stand 24.9 to 39 inches (640 to 1,000 mm) high at the shoulder, and weigh up to 176 pounds (80 kg).

The antlers of sika stags average in length from 11.7 to 25.7 inches (300 to 600 mm). The spikes of yearling stags are almost perfectly straight, while those of adult sika bend outward and slightly back. There are usually just three to five tines on each main beam, counting the tip of the main beam. The antlers are carried through the winter and shed in May. Unlike those of most deer, the sika's new antlers begin to grow at once, and their growth is complete in four months instead of five, as in most deer. Atypical antlers are seldom found in sika deer.

Sika deer have a coarse coat of hair. In winter, both sexes have a distinct dark mane of shaggy hair running from the top of the neck to the shoulders, with even longer hair hanging beneath the neck. The rest of the head is lighter in color than the mane, and slightly lighter in color than the rest of the body. Most summer coats are light tan with rows and blotches of white. (The tan does not have as much russet-red as that of the fallow deer, with which the sika could be confused.) Some sika subspecies have dark-brown coats.

In Siberia, sika deer are referred to as spotted deer, and their coats do have spots throughout their lives. However, an adult's winter coat has spots so indistinct that the spots are not visible at a distance. Siberians claim that the spots in the sika's winter coat are arranged differently than the spots in the summer coat.

All sika deer have an unusual white rump patch; the white part of the tail starts about three-quarters of the way down the tail, instead of encompassing the entire rump and tail as it does in most other deer species. The white extends down to the inguinal areas, with a little white on the body. There also is a little white on the inside of the deer's ears and a trace of white on the inside surface of the front legs. The large metatarsal glands are nestled in a tuft of white hair. Erector pili muscles allow the long rump hairs to be reversed, forming a pronounced rosette, when the deer are frightened or threatening a rival.

Sika deer usually shed their winter hair completely by the end of May. The winter coat has replaced the summer coat by the first of September.

Fat deposits found at the base of the sika's tail have been likened to the storage of fat in fat-tailed sheep and the humps of camels. It is suggested that this is a holdover from the time when these deer lived in much drier areas and the fat was broken down to produce internal water.

Habits: Sika deer are adaptable, and although they prefer forested areas with heavy underbrush, they can thrive in marshlands and swamps. On the Chincoteague Wildlife Refuge in Virginia, I saw them feeding in water like barasingha. Sika deer are strong swimmers and take readily to the water to escape predators or simply to travel to and from islands.

They are usually nocturnal in movement, but in protected areas they may feed until eight or nine in the morning, and again in the late afternoon. In their preferred forested areas, they feed upon twig tips and buds, leaves, berries, fruits, and acorns. In wet areas, they feed upon reeds, rushes, and emergent vegetation. When found along the seacoast, sika feed upon seaweed. In areas adjacent to farm crops, they often become a nuisance by damaging crops.

Like deer of all species, sika damage their habitat when they become overpopulated. In the United States, it has been found that where sika deer become established, populations of white-tailed deer decline.

Both species eat basically the same foods, and the whitetail can't withstand competition for the same food resources.

In forests, sika probably break down into family groups, but when feeding in open areas they congregate in herds in which the dominance social structure is readily seen. The oldest does usually lead the herd, both when escaping predators and when seeking food.

Sika deer run with a gallop and when pressed into a need for higher speed, resort to stotting, bouncing along with all four feet leaving the ground at one time, as if using a pogo stick. Because stotting is energy intensive, deer cannot keep it up for long periods of time and are quickly forced to hide in thick cover or to take to the water to escape predators.

Communication: Sika deer are very vocal, particularly during rutting season. They are credited with making ten different vocalizations, which is more than most deer species make. These include a soft whistling sound that females make, a bleating or neighing sound made by fawns, and the male's rutting-season call consisting of a loud whistle that ends with a roaring growl.

These deer make visual signs by making rubs on brush with their antlers. They deposit scent on their rubs from their preorbital glands. They use a head-high throat gesture of dominance, and signal aggressiveness and alertness to danger by flaring their rump hair.

Sika have large metatarsal glands, but it is not known just how they are used. They might be an aid in the marking of the stag's territory when it lies on the ground. That is the only time the metatarsals actually come in contact with anything.

During rutting season, males mark their selected territories by frequent pawing of the ground and then urinating in the scrapes.

Breeding: Rutting season extends from mid-September to mid-October, and I have witnessed the peak to be the first week in October. Adult stags try to gather a harem of four to six females. Rutting season is cha-

otic as the dominant male has to constantly run off the lesser males that continually try to cut a female from his harem. The stag's almost constant roaring is a warning, a challenge, and a way of venting frustration. While adult stags can chase off a smaller male with a bluff charge, they occasionally have to fight larger rivals.

Birth and Young: The gestation period for sika deer is about 210 days, with a fluctuation of a few days either way, depending upon the food that is available to the female during gestation.

Prior to giving birth, females establish a birthing territory, from which they drive their previous year's fawns and from which they attempt to keep out all other females. They usually give birth to a singleton; twins are exceedingly rare. Fawns typically weigh between 9.9 and 15.5 pounds (5 and 7 kg), average 22 inches (570 mm) in total length, and have a shoulder height of 19.5 inches (500 mm). Whereas with most deer the ratio of males to females is usually close to 50-50, with sika deer it appears to be closer to 60-40.

Fawns have spotted coats and stay hidden in their mother's birthing territory until they are two and a half to three weeks old. After this time they follow after the female and soon begin sampling the different types of vegetation that before long make up the bulk of their diet. At one year of age the young are almost as large as the females, and they become sexually mature at eighteen months of age.

In captivity, a sika deer lived to be twenty-five years, five months old.

Enemies: Dogs, lynx, leopard and the Siberian tiger all prey upon sika deer, but wolves are the principal predators.

Relationships with Humans: As always, humans have caused the sika's major decline, and over-hunting has decimated the sika's population in many areas. This was particularly true in Siberia after World War II, when many veterans returned from the Russian front and brought their rifles with them.

Thorold's Deer

Range: Thorold's deer (*Cervus albirostris*) inhabit the northeastern mountainous regions of Tibet and the headwaters area of the Yangtze River in southwestern China. It is an animal of the sub-alpine region, at home with the large-horned Asiatic sheep.

Description: The Thorold's deer is also known as the white-lipped deer because of the band of white hairs encircling its mouth and running behind its nostrils. It is also sometimes called Przewalski's deer, after Nikolai Mikhailovich Przewalski, a Russian explorer who first described the animal on his second trip to the Nan Shan Range in July 1876.

There are several special physical features about this deer that mark it as different from all others. A number of deer species have a section of hair on their brisket that points forward while all the rest of their hair points down or backward. Thorold's deer is the only species that has a patch of hair on its withers that points forward, giving it the appearance of having a small hump. The front of the hooves of Thorold's deer are steep and blunt looking, like the hooves of cattle, instead of having about a 35-degree slope like the hooves of most other deer. These hooves are an adaptation that allows the deer to scramble over rocks like a sheep.

The Thorold's deer is a stocky animal; its legs are shorter and thicker than are those of the other members of the *Cervus* family that live at lower elevations and on flatter terrain. They have a head and body length of about 88.5 inches (2,270 mm) and a tail length of about 5 inches (130 mm). Stags stand about 50.3 inches (1,290 mm) high at the shoulder, and weigh about 448 pounds (204 kg). There is a considerable dimorphism in this species, and females are considerably smaller than males, weighing about 275 pounds (125 kg).

The animals are brown during summer, with a cream-colored rump patch and tail and the aforementioned white around the muzzle and under the chin. The winter coat is lighter in color than the summer coat, probably because it is worn longer and gets bleached lighter by constant exposure to the sun. The hair of the winter coat is long, wavy, and has a dense undercoat of wool to allow the animals to withstand the bitter, biting cold they encounter at the high elevations—up to 16,733 feet (5,100 m)—where they are found. According to Valerius Geist, these animals may experience as few as twelve frost-free days in a year.

The Thorold's deer typically has a five-tined antler with brow tines that project forward at about a 90-degree angle. There is considerable distance between the brow and the second tine. The main beam is rather flattened and can be up to 54.6 inches (1,400 mm) in length.

These deer have both preorbital and metatarsal glands. Both male and female also have rudimentary maxillary canine teeth.

Habits: The Thorold's deer, like its counterpart the wapiti or American elk, is equally at home in mountainous forests and on open slopes. It has a wide muzzle, and its main foods are the various grasses and forbs that grow where the elevation and lack of moisture curtail the forests. It feeds most

The Thorold's deer is also known as the white-lipped deer because of the band of white hair encircling the end of its muzzle. (Photograph © Kenneth W. Fink/Photo Researchers)

heavily just after dawn and just before dark, similar to the feeding habits to of the wild Argalis sheep with which the deer often feeds. Also like the sheep, the deer heads for rocky outcroppings when danger threatens. Males—because they are larger, stronger, and faster than females—are able to feed farther from their favored rocky ledges. During winter, the deer seek out lower elevations or slopes where the wind is strong enough to blow off snow and reveal vegetation. The animals concentrate on feeding before the rut to maximize their body fat, which is needed if they are to survive the winter.

Thorold's deer, like the sheep with which they live, usually walk from place to place, though they do trot occasionally. They rarely run, but when pursued they can gallop at speeds up to 35 miles per hour (56 km). Because they are unaccustomed to galloping, it is a gait they cannot keep up but for a short distance.

Like the sheep, these deer depend more on their eyesight to detect danger than any of their other senses. In all mountainous areas, small pieces of rock break off almost constantly from the basic rock, forming talus slopes. Consequently, the deer are seldom disturbed by most noises they hear.

Living in such mountainous terrain, where one misstep may mean falling to their death, these deer are most active during the day and seldom move at night.

Communication: As open-area animals, Thorold's stags are very vocal. They roar frequently during breeding season. The roar starts on a low note, rises to a high-pitched scream, then tapers off as it drops down the scale to a low frequency. This roar is often given three to four times in a row. Stags also make a low-frequency growling.

Hinds have a high-pitched bark, which they give as a warning when they discover danger, or use when searching for a stray calf. Calves give high-pitched yelps when searching for their dam.

As any type of brush is rare in this area, stags do not hook the brush very often. They do run their antlers into the dirt, and the tips of their normally dark-brown antlers are worn white. The stags also use their antlers to gouge out chunks of turf when they make their wallows. Thorold's deer stags urinate both in their wallows and on their necks.

Breeding: Cold weather drives the deer down from their highest mountain ranges to areas they use in the winter. Thus the animals are concentrated for rutting season. The rut occurs in October, and stags round up hinds to form harems. There is much posturing and displaying by the males to attract the hinds and warn off rival males. Each animal knows his own exact body size and knows instantly how he stacks up against any of the other stags. This body language and bluffing serves to keep the need for actual fighting to a minimum. Stags make frequent use of wallows, and hinds also will often roll in the mud to coat their bodies. Hinds are in estrus for approximately twenty-four hours, and each hind is bred five or six times during that period.

Birth and Young: The gestation period for Thorold's deer is about 246 days. Usually only one spotted calf is born. The singletons are large, weighing about 18 to 19 pounds (8.1 to 8.6 kg). Calves are hidden in high grasses and hinds usually watch over them from a higher elevation some distance away. Hinds suckle their young three to four times in a twenty-four-hour period and then leave the area again. At the age of two weeks, the young start to follow after their mothers and often gather in nursery herds in which several hinds watch over the entire group while the rest of the mothers feed. This guarding and feeding is done on a rotation basis.

Young females are seldom bred until they are one and a half years old and, more frequently, not until they are two and a half years old. This delayed breeding is due mainly to the lack of a sufficiently nutritious diet. There is intense competition for forage, not only from wild sheep but also from yaks and domestic sheep herds of the nomadic people who live in the area.

Thorold's deer in captivity have lived to be nineteen years old.

Enemies: Thorold's deer do not encounter many natural predators. The snow leopard and wolf are the major predators, and both are scarce in the deer's range.

Relationship with Humans: Illegal poaching takes the greatest toll on Thorold's deer, while overgrazing by domestic herds limits the deer's reproductive capacity. There are a number of farms in China that keep large herds of Thorold's deer so that the stags' antlers can be removed while they are in velvet and sold for medicinal purposes.

Red Deer

Range: Red deer (*Cervus elaphus*) are found in Sweden, Norway, Scotland, eastern Europe, Spain, Corsica, Sardinia, northern Africa, Asia Minor, Kashmir, Chinese Turkistan, eastern Tibet, northern Afghanistan, and Russian Turkistan. The red deer has been introduced into New Zealand, Australia, Argentina, Chile, and Peru, and can also be found on some game ranches in the United States. There are twelve subspecies of red deer, and they are called Shou, Barbary, Hangul, Maral, Zarkland, Ruskharian, and other native and regional names, according to where they are found.

Description: Red deer are large, stately animals. Stags measure between 64.3 and 103.3 inches (1,650 to 2,650 mm) in head and body length and have a tail length of between 3.9 and 10.5 inches (100 and 270 mm), according to the subspecies. Stags stand 29.2 to 58.5 inches (750 to 1,500 mm) at the shoulder, and weigh between 165 and 748 pounds (75 and 340 kg). Hinds are about 25 percent smaller than stags, weighing between 124 and 561 pounds (56 and 254 kg).

The red deer's winter coat is dark brown in overall coloration with a prominent, creamy yellow rump patch. Stags have long, heavy, neck hair. Because they are basically open-area animals that are exposed to almost constant sunshine, red deer's winter coats bleach to a light tan color before they are shed in May. The summer coat is bright reddish-brown.

Red deer stags have large antlers, with the world record antlers measuring 49.3 inches (1,266 mm) in total length. A unique feature of the red deer's antlers in the European subspecies is that the fourth tine, commonly called the royal, on each main beam usually comprises a cluster of three to four points in the shape of a crown or basket. In this subspecies the main beams are massive; the circumference of the right main beam of a Norwegian stag is 9.9 inches (255 mm).

The red deer have large preorbital glands as well as metatarsal glands. They also have a gland located in the top of their tail. I can find no record in the red deer of the maxillary canine teeth.

Habits: The various subspecies of red deer are found in diverse types of habitat. Red deer in Scotland inhabit the heath-covered bald knobs of the highlands, primarily because agriculture has pushed them out of forests and better pasture areas of the lowlands. In Germany, red deer are almost exclusively found in for-

ests. In eastern Europe, they may be found in riverine basins, where vegetation is much more nutritious than in other habitats; this explains why stags there have the largest bodies and antlers of all the subspecies. As most island animals have restricted diets, the red deer of Corsica and Sardinia are small.

The comparatively wide muzzle shows that red deer evolved primarily as a grazing animal, regardless of what it is found eating today. Grasses are the mainstay of most red deer diets, but browse makes up much of the diet of those red deer that live in the forest.

Red deer are muscular animals with efficient lungs, which allow them to run fast for a considerable length of time. They can run over 35 miles per hour (56 kph). In the days when red deer were hunted with horses and hounds, hunters frequently had to use three to five horses to bring a stag to bay. The powerful haunches of red deer enable them to easily jump over fallen trees and bushes.

Where possible, red deer of the forests move to higher terrain in summertime because they are easily stressed by heat. The animals begin to move upward to traditional calving grounds at least a month before calves are dropped. Hinds start the upward movement several weeks before stags, and hurry as if they want to be sure to get there with time to spare. Stags move upward at a more leisurely pace, even though they have a greater distance to travel as they seek out the highest meadows in the area. The sexes stay in separate herds for about seven months out of the year.

Red deer have a matriarchal society, and the female herd is led by one of the oldest hinds. In any herd there may be several matriarchs. This can be seen when the herd starts off in one direction following a matriarch, then stops and heads off in another direction, following a different matriarch. The herd doesn't necessarily split; the first leader may simply turn around and follow after the rest, with the herd remaining as a cohesive group. Matriarchs are seldom challenged, but the oldest are followed so long as they are still able to bear a calf each year. In the rare event they become old enough to become barren, they lose their status as a herd leader. A hind's own young will often follow her until they are three years old.

Stag herds never become as large as hind herds; although the sex ratio at birth is about 50-50, males suffer higher mortality rates. Young males are more adventuresome, more active, more curious, and get into more trouble than females. Stags are not as alert to the possibility of danger as are the lead hinds, nor

Red deer stags peel the velvet from their antlers during the end of August and the first part of September. (Photograph by Leonard Lee Rue III)

are they as concerned for their herd's welfare. Stag herds are more loosely structured; there is no "leader" male, although there may be a dominant male that does not necessarily lead.

Red deer feed primarily at dawn, at about 11 A.M. and again just before dark. They may feed a little at night, but except during rutting season, they are not very active at night.

There are several advantages to being in a herd. A single animal will usually lie with its back to the wind, so it can smell the scent of every creature upwind, while its eyes scan for danger downwind. This precludes the possibility of predators sneaking up on the herd undetected. The larger the herd, the more noses, eyes, and ears there are on guard. With a large herd, some animals are always awake while the others are sleeping. When a herd runs off in a mass, it is difficult for a predator to select one animal to attack.

Communication: The most commonly heard sound of red deer is the staccato bark of an alarmed matriarch. This short, sharp bark will instantly cause every deer that hears it to become alert. All activity ceases as the other members seek what it was that disturbed their leader. The matriarch's body language also conveys danger—her head is held as high as possible. The bark is just a warning. The herd will not dash for cover unless the matriarch does, then all will follow. Hinds also bark to locate a misplaced calf, but that call has more of a yelp to it. Calves make a bleating yelp.

Stags are usually silent for most of the year, but during rutting season they made a deep guttural roaring almost constantly, day and night. The sound is quite different from the bugling of the North American wapiti, because the mouth is held in a more closed fashion, the lower teeth are not seen, and the cheeks are used to form a resonating chamber. F. Frazer Darling made an interesting observation in his extensive study of red deer. He claims that although the stags' roar is much louder than the hind's alarm bark, the hind's bark can be heard at a much greater distance because of its higher pitch and tonality.

Stags make visual signs by debarking brush and saplings with their antlers to expose the white inner bark. Red deer stags urinate on their long neck hairs and make use of wallows in self-advertisement. With their antlers, they plow up the turf in wet areas, then use their antlers and their feet to turn the wet soil into mud. They urinate in the mud to make it more odorous and liquid. They then roll about in the mud, liberally coating their long neck hair and their bodies with it. They frequently rub their necks against evergreen trees to deposit the mud and their scent on the trees, and also to get the resin from the trees on their neck. All of these odors are attractive to the hinds as sexual stimulants.

Breeding: The rut, for most red deer, occurs from mid-September through mid-October. The dominant stag gathers a number of hinds together on a piece of territory that he tries to defend against all other males. A stag loses considerable weight at this time as he is forced to continually herd hinds back into his own personal territory, while at the same time trying to keep all other adult males away. (Yearling stags are tolerated if they make no advances toward any hinds.) Where possible, the stag will try to select a territory with easy access to water. Although the stag has little time to eat, he requires a high daily consumption of water to maintain his constant running, chasing, fighting, and self-marking (urinating on his neck and making wallows).

The harems are largest early in the season because the testosterone levels rise at a slightly different pace in adult males. Those stags whose testosterone levels peak first and who gather huge harems early, gradually lose some of their hinds as other males' testosterone levels peak. Stags less than four years old can seldom hold a harem. Stags peak in fitness between five and ten years of age.

Hinds are in estrus for twenty-four to twenty-eight hours. A stag is constantly sniffing the urine or the vulva of every female in his harem, searching for the pheromones that will denote a hind's readiness to breed. The male courts the female by licking her head, body, and vulva. He often lays his head across her back. The estrus female often reciprocates by rubbing her body against the male and licking his head. The stag usually prevents an estrus hind from getting any rest. If she lies down, he may strike at her with one of his forefeet or jab her lightly with his antlers to get her back up on her feet. After he has bred her several times and her estrus period passes, the stag completely ignores that hind as he searches for the next estrus female.

The antlers of this young red deer stag are just starting to form the "crown" that will qualify him as a "royal" in the coming years. (Photograph by Leonard Lee Rue III)

Birth and Young: The gestation period for red deer is between 230 and 238 days. The hind leaves the herd several days before giving birth and seeks out an isolated spot where she drops her calf. Calves have a spotted coat at birth because they are "hiders." A single calf is the norm; twins are exceedingly rare. Calves weigh between 11.5 and 15.9 pounds (5 and 7 kg) at birth. They can walk within an hour, and the hind then leads them away from the birthing spot and hides them in safe cover. Calves can follow after their mothers in three to four days, and are soon sampling all the types of vegetation she is eating.

Calves grow rapidly and lose their spots at about three months of age. They are usually weaned at four months, but may nurse for a longer time. The young stay with their mother until she gives birth the following year and then, as yearlings, will rejoin her. Young males usually leave to join bachelor groups at one to one and a half years of age.

Red deer have been known to live twenty-seven years.

Enemies: Wolves, bears, tigers, and leopards are the main predators of the red deer.

Relationship with Humans: The red deer is to the Europeans what the white-tailed deer is to Americans—the most important game animal on the continent. It is estimated that there are one million red deer in Europe. It is the most sought after, studied, and managed of all of the animals in Eurasia. Just as red deer were once reserved only for royalty, one must still be rich today to hunt them, because most of the animals, even the wild ones, live in restricted private forests and preserves. There are a number of preserves where the animals are kept so their velvet-covered antlers can be collected at the proper time to be used in the medicinal trade.

During rutting season, red deer stags frequent muddy wallows, as the water line on this one's body shows. (Photograph by Leonard Lee Rue III)

Red deer stags gather together harems of hinds and their calves during rutting season. (Photograph by Leonard Lee Rue III)

A grouping of fine red deer stags just prior to rutting season. (Photograph by Leonard Lee Rue III)

Wapiti/Elk

The name *wapiti* is derived from the Shawnee Indian word meaning "white-rumped." (The actual word that the Shawnee used for this animal was *wabete*.) *Wapiti* is used in scientific circles to avoid using the word *elk*, which is the commonly used name for *Cervus canadensis* in North America. The German word *Elch* and Norwegian word *elg*, with which the word *elk* might be confused, are used by these Europeans to refer to their moose.

There are eleven living subspecies of wapiti and two that have become extinct. The American wapiti, the prototype for which the species was named, became extinct by the end of the 1800s. The Merriam's wapiti became extinct between 1902 and 1906. Today there are four subspecies of wapiti in North American and seven subspecies in Asia.

Range: At one time, one or some of the six subspecies of wapiti were found in all of the contiguous forty-eight states except Arizona and the New England states. Over-hunting then annihilated the wapiti east of the Great Plains and severely restricted their population in even the mountain areas. Better game laws saved the species and reintroduction has established the wapiti in many of its former ranges. Today wapiti are found in Washington, Oregon, California, Idaho, Montana, Wyoming, Colorado, Nevada, Utah, Arizona, New Mexico, Texas, Oklahoma, Kansas, South Dakota, North Dakota, Minnesota, Michigan, Pennsylvania, and Florida. They have recently been reintroduced to Kentucky, Tennessee, and North Carolina, and were introduced in Alaska. Wapiti are also found in the six westernmost Canadian provinces.

In Asia the seven wapiti subspecies are found in the mountain regions of Kazakhstan; Kyrgyzstan; Inner and Outer Mongolia; southeastern Siberia; North Korea; north, central, and southeast China; and Tibet.

Description: The wapiti species of North America and northern Asia are larger than those of southern Asia. Basically all of these animals fall within the following size ranges. Wapiti have a head and body length of 64.3 to 103.3 inches (1,650 to 2,650 mm), with a tail length of 3.9 to 10.5 inches (100 to 270 mm). They stand from 29.2 to 58.5 inches (750 to 1,500 mm) high at the shoulder and weigh 165 to 770 pounds (75 to 340 kg). Wapiti bulls are larger than wapiti cows by about 25 percent.

Wapiti have stocky bodies, but the long legs of a cursorial runner. They can easily run more than 35 miles per hour (56 kph) and keep up that speed for a considerable length of time. Despite their weight, they are good jumpers. I, personally, once saw a bull jump an 8-foot (2 m) fence.

The huge antlers of the bulls are the crowning

Right: The Tule elk of California is the smallest subspecies of wapiti found in North America. (Photograph by Leonard Lee Rue III)

Facing page: The Roosevelt elk is the largest subspecies of elk found in North America. This big bull weighs about 900 pounds (409 kg). (Photograph by Uschi Rue)

Map of wapiti range in Asia

glory of the wapiti. The antlers are often five feet (1,524 mm) in length and have up to a 53-inch (1,346 mm) inside spread. Adult bulls usually have six tines on each antler, with exceptionally good bulls having seven tines on each. One bull that I saw in Jasper, Alberta, Canada, had eight tines on one antler and nine tines on the other.

Many North American wapiti, both male and female, have well-developed maxillary canine teeth that have up to .75 inch (19 mm) of the tooth exposed. These teeth were greatly desired by the Amerindians for decorative purposes and some of the women's dresses had hundreds of teeth sewn on for decoration. The teeth were also used as talismans by members of the Benevolent & Protective Order of Elks, and are still a great trophy for hunters today.

Wapiti have well-developed preorbital glands, which they flare widely when excited, and glands on the outside of their hind legs. There is another gland under the skin surrounding the tail vertebra, which gives the stumpy tail its slightly swollen appearance. They do not have tarsal or interdigital glands.

The basic body color is brownish-gray. The head and neck of both sexes is covered with long hair of a rich, chestnut-brown color. The short tail and the large rump patch are a creamy white, and the rump patch has a dark border. The belly hair is almost black and the legs are very dark. Females are lighter in overall color and their neck hair is shorter than that of males.

Winter hair bleaches in the spring sun and molts into a summer coat in May. The summer coat is a bright reddish-tan and has no dense undercoat. The molt to the winter coat starts in August. The winter coat has a dense woolly undercoat that provides the warmth needed for the animals to survive the bitter mountain winter.

Habits: Wapiti are primarily grazing animals and have a comparatively wide muzzle. They feed mainly on grasses and forbs for as long as this type of vegetation is available. In the forested areas, they browse on woody twigs and feed upon many types of tree leaves, even those that have fallen from the tree. In winter they eat many different types of conifers. I have often seen big bulls stand upright on their hind legs and use their antlers to break off high branches that they can't reach with their mouths. In winter they also scar aspen trees when, using their lower teeth, they gouge off long strips of bark for food.

Wapiti are basically grazers, which means they are also herd animals and as such, have a great deal of social interaction. Except during breeding season, or if they are forced to seek food together during winter months, bulls and cows live in separate herds and usually live at separate elevations.

As soon as the snows have melted enough to allow passage, cows and their previous year's calves head from the lowlands to higher mountain meadows, where the cows will give birth to new calves. The bulls follow along at a much more leisurely rate and then pass the cows, heading for the highest, windswept, mountain meadows. The new grasses in such places are nutritious, and bulls need all the nutrition they can get to promote the growth of their massive antlers. The wind at the higher elevations also cuts down on the annoyance of blood-sucking insects. Even wapiti living in the Plains states of the United States seek out the highest hills in their area.

Wapiti start to feed before it gets light in the morning and continue until about 8 A.M. They will then seek shade in the forests until about 11 A.M., when they feed again, usually near their bedding area. They are active again from about 5 P.M. until dark. They then bed for the night in the meadows in which they are feeding. Wapiti do not move about much at night, except during rutting season, when the bulls are active twenty-four hours a day.

Wapiti stay in high mountain meadows until around the first of September, when the cows start to drift to lower pasturage on their traditional breeding grounds. The bulls drift down slower, but an early season snowfall will send all of the animals streaming down from the high meadows. After rutting season, additional snow, strong wind, and plummeting temperatures push them even lower into the valleys, where they will spend the winter.

Wapiti, like all *Cervids*, are a matriarchal society, with the herds led by the oldest, most experienced cows. These matriarchs determine when, where, and how the herds do anything, except for about three weeks during the rut. During that short period, the dominant bulls usurp the matriarchs' leadership and

This elk calf already has its heavy coat of winter hair. (Photograph by Len Rue Jr.)

determine when and where the herd will feed and where they will bed for the day. Bulls execute all their decisions with none-too-gentle herding activities. The bull's herding does not provide protection from predators; it is done to insure his sexual gratification. When danger threatens, the cows are on their own and the matriarchs decide the course of action. When danger is past, a bull will round up whichever cows he can and herd them back to his personal territory.

Communication: Bull wapiti are rightfully famous for their high-pitched bugling; they shatter the stillness of the night with a bellow that can be heard for miles. To me, it is one of the most fantastic wildlife sounds that I know. I have heard elk bugle thousands of times, and the sound still thrills me to the very core of my being; it's primordial. The call starts off low, rapidly ascends to a high-pitched scream, and then slides down the scale. In most cases, with the biggest bulls the call is followed with five or six resonant gruntings that come from the bottom of the bull's diaphragm.

The most commonly heard call of the cow is the high-pitched yelp. The yelp can be either an alarm bark or a searching call for a lost calf, according to the inflection in the tone.

Scent plays an extremely important role in wapiti communication. Bulls saturate their long neck hair by fully extending and palpitating their penis as they squirt a steady stream of urine between their legs. With their long fourth, or royal, antler tines, they tear up chunks of turf in moist areas and use their forefeet to paw the damp soil into a muddy wallow. They urinate copiously in the wallow to make the mud more

A bull elk's bugle call is a challenge to other males and an attraction to females. (Photograph by Uschi Rue)

liquid. Then they lie down in the mud and roll from side to side, liberally coating their necks and bodies. In creating olfactory signposts, bulls trash pine saplings with their antlers, breaking off the branches and often the top, and stripping off the dark outer bark, exposing the bright white inner bark. In the course of just one rutting season, a dominant bull will kill dozens of pine saplings around the edge of a meadow. (This is actually beneficial as it prevents the forest from encroaching on the grassland, which the animals need for feeding.) In trashing the saplings, the bulls are delineating their territories. The odor on the broken trunks is a warning to rival bulls and an invitation to the cows. The trashing of the saplings also strengthens bulls' neck muscles, providing them with a tremendous physical work out, and is a means of working off their frustrations when the cows aren't yet ready to accept their advances. The bulls also love to rub their necks on mature pines to get the resins on their neck hairs. At this time, bulls reek and can be smelled at a considerable distance.

When a bull is herding a cow, he holds his head parallel to his body, which allows his antlers to project back and down either side of his body. He turns his head away from the direction in which he wants the cow to go, but she knows exactly what he wants her to do and she does it or gets gored for being difficult. When two big bulls challenge each other, they use the same position of the head, but they run parallel to each other, separated by a distance of about 20 to 30 feet (6 to 10 m). With all the precision of a minuet, they run for a distance of perhaps 300 feet (92 m), turn and retrace their steps, then turn again. One or the other bull may suddenly stop to thrash a bush or sapling or to tear up turf with his antlers in a displaced threat aggression, while the other bull waits for him. Both of the bulls may then bugle loudly and either parallel walk again or simply trot off in different directions. Sparring is commonly done by young bulls; sincere fighting is rare among dominant bulls.

Breeding: Five-tined bulls frequently gather harems together, but they can seldom hold them, as they usually are displaced by bigger, more mature bulls. Harems of fifty cows and their calves are commonly seen in the second week of September, but the harems become smaller as more of the dominant bulls come down from the high meadows and the competition becomes greater. Twenty to twenty-five cows and calves constitute an average harem. Many of the big dominant bulls will lay claim to the same piece of territory each rutting season for a number of years.

The harem master is constantly checking every cow. As he runs from one cow to another, he flicks his tongue out rapidly. Coming up behind the cow, the bull will sniff her vulva or her urine and will then raise his head, curl back his upper lip, and flehmen. This allows him to process the cow's pheromones to see if she is ready to breed. If the bull attempts to mount a cow that is not in estrus, she will either run off in a slinking position or keep turning so she is parallel to the bull, but facing the opposite direction. In frustration, the bull bugles frequently.

When a cow is ready to be bred, she will stand for the bull while he licks her head, her body, and her vulva. She will allow him to lay his head along her back. The bull usually makes a number of false mountings before he finally inserts his penis. The bull makes a few thrusts and then the copulatory thrust wherein he achieves the deepest penetration and ejaculates. When making the final thrust, the bull throws his head vertically up and back and his hind feet often leave the ground. After breeding the cow several times, the bull leaves her and searches for his next conquest.

Occasionally in courtship a cow will mount a bull.

Birth and Young: The gestation period for American wapiti is from 245 to 250 days, with most calves born the last week of May or in early June. A single spotted calf is the norm; twins are exceedingly rare. Singleton calves weigh from 30 to 40 pounds (14 to 18 kg) at birth. Any calf weighing only 25 pounds (11 kg) has little chance of survival.

Calves are usually dropped in some secluded area that the cow deems safe. A calf can walk within an hour, at which time it is led from the birth area to a safer hiding place, away from the blood and amniotic fluids that seeped out during birthing. The cow stands guard from a distance, returning to nurse the calf three or more times in twenty-four hours. Within two weeks, calves can run, and their mothers bring them to a central location as the herds reform. Cows often leave their calves in nursery groups guarded by several cows, while the rest of the mothers go off to feed. Calves are nursed for three months or longer. I have videotaped a fifteen-month-old bull still nursing his mother whenever she would allow it, even though she was also nursing a three-month-old calf.

Calves lose their spots at about three months of age. They stay with their mothers until they leave to give birth to their own calves. Young females usually breed at sixteen months of age and stay with their mother's herd. Young males either drift away, or are driven away, to form their own peer groups or to join the bull herds.

One bull that had been tagged by the U.S. Biological Survey (part of the U.S. Fish and Wildlife Service) was twenty-five years old when shot.

Enemies: Adult wapiti in North America are preyed upon by wolves, cougars, and bears. Calves are also preyed upon by golden eagles, coyotes, bobcats, and feral dogs. In Asia, tigers, bears, and wolves are the main predators.

Diseases of different types play havoc with wapiti. One disease that is causing great concern today is chronic wasting disease, which started in pen-raised animals and spread to wild stock. The parasitic meningeal brainworm *Tenuis* can be spread from white-tailed deer, which have developed immunity to it, to wapiti, and it often proves fatal to wapiti.

Relationship with Humans: The future of North American wapiti is secure, despite the constant habitat erosion caused by human development of the land. The National Elk Foundation of Missoula, Montana, is doing an excellent job preserving critical core lands and fostering the reintroduction of animals to much of their former range. Thankfully, the elk is proving to be more resilient and adaptable than was previously believed.

In Asia, wapiti populations are declining because of over-hunting and increased habitat destruction.

A rutting bull elk will tear up the turf with his antlers to start a wallow (above). He urinates on his neck hairs and then on the ground to make it more liquid. (facing page, top and middle). Finally, he rolls in the wallow to coat his hair with the scent-laden mud (facing page, bottom). (Above and facing page top, photographs by Uschi Rue; facing page middle by Leonard Lee Rue III; facing page bottom by Len Rue Jr.)

After tearing the bark off this pine tree, the bull elk will rub his scent on the wood and get the pine sap on his neck hairs. (Photograph by Len Rue Jr.)

This is an exceptionally fine Rocky Mountain bull elk because his antlers have seven tines on each main beam. (Photograph by Len Rue Jr.)

During rutting season, each bull elk will gather together as large a harem of cows and calves as he can defend against rival males. (Photograph by Leonard Lee Rue III)

Above: In flehmening, as this bull elk is doing, animals pull scent into their vomeronasal organ, located in the roof of their mouth. The gland then sends signals to the brain, allowing the animal to analyze and identify the scent. (Photograph by Uschi Rue)

Left: In courtship, bull elk frequently caress the cows to stimulate them to breed. (Photograph by Uschi Rue)

This Rocky Mountain cow elk thoroughly washes her just-born calf. This act not only cleans the calf of amniotic fluids, which may attract predators, but also imprints the calf upon the cow and the cow upon the calf. (Photograph by Uschi Rue)

Although most weaning is finished by four months of age, this elk cow still allows her five-month-old calf to nurse. (Photograph by Uschi Rue)

Thousands upon thousands of wapiti spend the winter on the National Elk Range outside Jackson, Wyoming. Some elk have traveled more than 75 miles (121 km) in migration to reach the refuge. Such large numbers of elk can survive all winter in the refuge because of daily supplemental feeding by the federal government. The elk stay in the refuge until about April, when 75 percent of them head for their summer range. The remaining 25 percent of the elk spend their summer in ranges adjacent to the refuge. (Photograph by Uschi Rue)

Peré David's Deer

Range: The original range of Peré David's deer (*Elaphurus davidianus*) was the swamps and marshes of north and central China. From the scanty records available, the deer ceased to live in the wilds somewhere around 220 A.D. Thankfully, before this time, several herds were rounded up and imported to the Imperial Hunting Grounds of the emperor on the outskirts of what was then called Peking (now Beijing). The park was surrounded by a high wall that was 44.7 miles (72 km) long. Guards kept everyone out of the park. No one except the emperors and their retinues even knew about the deer until in 1865 a French Jesuit priest, Armand David, bribed a guard to let him just look over the wall. To his surprise he saw a herd of 120 deer. Father David took note of the odd deer, thinking they were a type of reindeer. Through further bribery, the priest obtained two skins of the deer, which he sent back to France with his description of what he had seen. The French zoologist Henry Milne-Edwards wrote the first scientific paper on the deer, based on the skins and Father David's observations. Edwards named the deer after Peré David (*Peré* is French for *father*).

Later, some of the deer were given to zoos in Paris, London, and Berlin. When a catastrophic flood in 1895 wiped out all the original deer in China, it was the deer at the Duke of Bedford's private park at Woburn, England, that became the nucleus for all the breeding stock. The breeding program was eminently successful, and many zoos have raised enough of these deer that herds have been returned to China, and some have even been returned to the wild there.

Description: The Chinese call the deer *Sen-Pou-Siang*, which basically translates to mean "Four-Unlike." They say that the Peré David's deer has the antlers of a stag, the feet of a cow, the neck of a camel, and the tail of a donkey. I have studied deer all of my life, and the Peré David's deer is the oddest looking deer I've ever seen.

Peré David's deer are big. They have a head and body length of 71.3 to 84.2 inches (1,830 to 2,160 mm). They have the longest tail of any deer in the world, measuring between 8.5 and 13.8 inches (220 and 355 mm). These deer stand 47.5 to 53.4 inches (1,220 to 1,370 mm) at the shoulder. The average weight for an adult male is 470.8 pounds (214 kg), while adult females average 349.8 pounds (159 kg).

The summer coats of these deer range from tan to deep reddish-brown. In August they begin to develop a winter coat, which is much grayer, and has a dense undercoat of wavy wool that provides them with excellent insulation. They have no rump patch, but G. Kenneth Whitehead makes note of whorls of hair on the deer's sacrum and on either side of its neck.

Peré David's deer have the longest preorbital

A male Peré David's deer courts a female during the rut. The Peré David's deer is very odd looking. It has the longest tail of any deer and its antler tines project backward instead of forward. (Photograph © Erwin & Peggy Bauer)

glands of any deer I've ever seen, and the bare skin around each gland makes it appear even larger. These deer do not have tarsal, metatarsal, or interdigital glands.

Their hooves are large and their dewclaws are long enough to touch the ground. Their feet look like those of caribou and reindeer, which have splayed feet to walk on snow, while the Peré David's feet are adapted to walk on mud.

The antlers of Peré David's deer are unique in that they appear to have been put on the stag's head backward. About 8 inches (203 mm) above the burr, the antlers bifurcate so that the main beams diverge widely on each side of the head. The main beams reach a length of 25 to 32 inches (720 to 840 mm) each. The tines emanating from these beams point downward instead of up, as other deer's do. Peré David's deer and roe deer are the only two species of deer to grow antlers during wintertime. These deer have rudimentary maxillary canine teeth.

Habits: Peré David's deer have wide muzzles, denoting that they are grazing animals. They feed mainly on grasses, reeds, and rushes of the marshy areas they inhabit. These deer are strong swimmers, as would be expected of animals that live around water. They walk with a rather stiff gait and are not fast runners, with a top speed of about 18.6 miles per hour (30 kph). They are herd animals with a matriarchal society. The sexes are in separate herds except during breeding season. They mainly feed early and late in the day, although they may move about and feed at any time.

Communication: Peré David's deer are not very vocal except during breeding season, when the stags roar frequently. Their roar is deep-pitched and choppy, not drawn out like that of the wapiti. The hinds have a high-pitched, barking yelp; the calves make a similar sound, but lack the volume.

Stags self-advertise by urinating on their long neck hair. Their method of doing this is different from all other deer in that they swing their penises from side to side horizontally, saturating their chest, legs, and neck hair. A stag will dig out wallows in the mud, urinate copiously in the hollow created, then lie down and roll in the mud, plastering himself thoroughly. Stags also rub their preorbital glands and neck hairs on saplings and trees in the area. As they live in marshes, where the grasses are longer than normal, stags will frequently tear up clumps of long grass and carry the grass around on their antlers. This act may be done to make their antlers appear larger, thus intimidating rival stags.

Breeding: Breeding season begins in late June, when the herds of hinds gather into harems on traditional grounds. A dominant male will join each harem and attempt to keep other males out of the area, although he does not have to herd the cows together to keep them in the area. There is some sparring, parallel walking, and occasionally some fights. Stags sometimes fight by standing upright and striking out with their forefeet. Through July, as the dominant stags become exhausted, they leave the hinds and are replaced by younger males.

Peré David's deer have been crossbred with red deer at the Berlin Zoo and have produced fertile offspring, showing that *Elaphurus* is closely related to *Cervus*.

Birth and Young: The gestation period for Peré David's deer is long, averaging about 283 days. Just prior to giving birth, the hind leaves the herd and seeks out a safe haven. One or two spotted calves is the norm. At birth calves weigh about 24.2 pounds (11 kg). Calves stay hidden, relying on their cryptic coloration to allow them to remain unseen. A hind watches over her calves from a distance, coming back to nurse them about four times in a twenty-four-hour period. By one week of age, the calves start to follow after the hind, which soon leads them to join the herd. Young are nursed for about four months and they lose their spots about the same time they are weaned. They do not become sexually mature until after two years of age.

A Peré David's deer is known to have lived to be twenty-three years, three months old.

Enemies: Except for one herd that has been returned to the wild in China and is closely guarded, there are no wild Peré David's deer, and so they are never preyed upon.

Relationship with Humans: It was humans who brought Peré David's deer to the brink of extinction and humans who brought the deer back. There are now several thousand Peré David's deer in eighty-four captive herds throughout the world.

Mule Deer

Range: There are eleven subspecies of mule deer, three of which are classified as black-tailed deer. Mule deer are found in all of the western United States and Canada from Mexico north to the Yukon. Mule deer are primarily deer of mountainous regions. Black-tailed deer are found from Alaska's southeastern panhandle down along the coastal regions of British Columbia, Washington, Oregon, and California.

Description: The mule deer (*Odocoileus hemionus*) is a stocky animal with a heavy body and stout legs. A full-grown buck will stand 40 to 42 inches (1,016 to 1,066 mm) high at the shoulder and measure about 78 inches (1,981 mm) in overall length. The average weight is 175 to 200 pounds (79 to 91 kg), although many large specimens reach 300 to 450 pounds (136 to 204 kg). Average does weigh about one-third less than males. The record weight is a Colorado mule deer buck taken in 1938 that weighed 522.75 pounds (237 kg).

The black-tailed deer is smaller, standing about 38 inches (965 mm) at the shoulder and measuring about 60 inches (1,152 mm) in overall length. It weighs up to 150 pounds (68 kg), but exceptionally large bucks weigh over 300 pounds (136 kg).

The mule deer was given its name because its large ears look like those of a mule. The ears are about 11 inches (279 mm) in length and about 6 inches (152 mm) wide. The oversized ears allow the deer to hear danger coming from a greater distance and act as thermoregulators, helping cool the deer's blood in hot weather.

The mule deer's tail is round and white, except for a 2-inch (51 mm) black tip. The upper tail surface of the black-tailed deer is solid black, hence its name. Neither of these deer can flare the hairs on their tails.

Like most deer, in the summer the mule deer's hair color is a reddish-brown. The winter coat of hollow guard hairs is a somber grayish-brown. There is a dense, grayish, woolly undercoat that provides excellent insulation against the subzero temperatures to which these deer are often exposed. Most of these deer

Most mule deer subspecies live in the high mountains of the western United States. (Photograph by Leonard Lee Rue III)

Map of mule deer range in North America

The mule deer got its name from its exceptionally large ears. (Photograph by Uschi Rue)

have a black "skullcap" extending down to their eye level.

These deer have forehead, preorbital, interdigital, tarsal, and metatarsal scent glands. The blacktail's metatarsal gland is a 3-inch (76 mm) crescent, and the mule deer's metatarsal gland is S-shaped and 5 inches (127 mm) long. (Compare these to the whitetail's metatarsal gland, which is 1 inch [25 mm] long.)

Mule deer's antlers are unique in that the main beams bifurcate and then split again so that it looks like the buck has two slingshots on each antler. The brow tines are short, seldom getting to be 3 inches (76 mm) long.

Habits: Most of these deer spend their summer in mountainous areas, and snow forces them to seek lower elevations in the fall. Some mule deer travel as much as 100 miles (160 km) in migration. Blacktails don't travel as far, but snow will force them down to the seacoast, where they often have to survive on seaweed and kelp. Bucks keep separate from does except during breeding season or if they are forced to spend the winter together.

Both mulies and blacktails walk, trot, and gallop, but to escape danger they bound off stotting, with all four feet leaving the ground at one time. This gait is tiring, but it allows the deer to efficiently bound up steep hillsides and escape. Both types of deer have been clocked at 35 miles per hour (59 kph) and can clear 8-foot (2 m) fences.

These deer eat mainly grasses, forbs, berry bushes, berries, fruits, and twigs, according to the season and the vegetation available. They mainly feed early in the morning and late in the afternoon. In the hotter regions of their range, they will feed only when the shadows are long and the temperature is cooler. They like to retire to cliffsides or hillsides where, from some shady spot, they can look out over great distances to watch for danger. The mule deer is more aggressive than the whitetail in making a defense against dogs and coyotes.

Communication: When mule deer are alarmed, they snort by blasting air through their noses, producing a whistling sound. During the rut, bucks make a coughing-grunting sound. When they call, they make a deep, raspy, blatting sound like that of an old domestic sheep. Does make a similar sound that has a higher pitch. Fawns bleat like lambs.

Bucks make rubs on trees and deposit scent. They also make scrapes and deposit scent. They use body language, including the "hard stare," which denotes aggression, to intimidate rivals.

Breeding: The rut starts at the end of October, at which time the buck's neck starts to swell. The buck gathers a small harem, and the peak of the breeding is done the latter part of November. When the ranges of the mule deer and the whitetail overlap, there is hybridization. Usually the cross is between a whitetail buck and a mulie doe. Although the bucks of both species will chase an estrus doe, the whitetail is a much more persistent suitor and usually wins out. Although each crossing results in fertile offspring, the offspring fall prey to predators more easily because they can't stot as well as mule deer, nor can they run as far and as fast as whitetail.

The gestation period for mule deer is approximately 210 days, with twins the norm. Fawns have spotted coats and are kept hidden for the first two to three weeks of life. Fawns are weaned in three months, lose their spots at four months, and follow closely after their mothers until they are almost one year old, at which time she will drive them off before giving birth to new fawns. Mule deer have a matriarchal society, and although they often break down into familial groups, they usually associate in larger herds than do white-tailed deer.

The oldest mule deer on record was a doe in British Columbia that lived to be twenty-two years old.

Enemies: Feral dogs, coyotes, wolves, lynx, cougars, and bears all take mule deer whenever the opportunity presents itself. Cougars are probably mule deer's number-one predator. All creatures are subject to diseases and parasites, but a new viral infection known as chronic wasting disease has begun to take a toll on both mule deer and elk in Colorado, Wyoming, Nebraska, and Kansas.

Relationship with Humans: The mule deer is eagerly sought after by trophy hunters because of its magnificent antlers. Over the past two decades, the population of mule deer has dropped from 6 million animals to around 4 million. Part of this drop is due to hunting pressure, but a greater cause is the destruction of the mule deer's habitat by land development.

In addition, the mule deer faces threats from within the deer family. As the white-tailed deer invades the mule deer's range, it transmits the brainworm *Tenuis* to the mulie; the white-tailed deer has developed immunity to it, but the mule deer has not. Between interbreeding and this disease, the mule deer's population will continue to decline as the whitetail's increases.

As a species, mule deer bucks are larger bodied than white-tailed bucks. (Photograph by Uschi Rue)

Mule deer bucks usually weigh between 200 and 300 pounds (91 and 136 kg). The record weight for a mule deer buck was noted in 1938 in Colorado, with a buck that weighed 522.75 pounds (237.3 kg). The rack of the average mule deer buck is 24 to 28 inches (610 to 711 mm) in length. The world-record mule deer has a left main beam that is 30.125 inches (765.1 mm) in length. (Photograph by Len Rue Jr.)

In stotting, mule and black-tailed deer bound along as if on springs, with all four feet leaving the ground at once. (Photograph by Len Rue Jr.)

Mule deer gather in larger herds than do white-tailed deer. (Photograph by Leonard Lee Rue III)

Facing page: Unlike whitetails, mule deer often stop and look back to see what it was that disturbed them. (Photograph by Uschi Rue)

Left: The first snows of winter push the mule deer down from their high summer range to the warmer valleys below. (Photograph by Leonard Lee Rue III)

This mule deer buck is in the process of rubbing the velvet from his antlers. (Photograph by Uschi Rue)

Having removed the bark from the sapling, this mule deer buck is rubbing his forehead scent glands against the inner wood. (Photograph by Len Rue Jr.)

The western black-tailed bucks are usually smaller than the bucks of the northern white-tailed subspecies. (Photograph by Leonard Lee Rue III)

Notice the all-black upper-tail surface of this young black-tailed deer. (Photograph by Uschi Rue)

At the age of three and a half months, this black-tailed fawn is losing its spotted natal coat. (Photograph by Uschi Rue)

A black-tailed doe is unable to signal danger to her cohorts by flaring her tail as a white-tailed doe would do. (Photograph by Leonard Lee Rue III)

Left: These wolves are feeding on a mule deer buck. Wolves throughout the world, wherever they are found, are a major predator of any deer in the area. (Photograph by Uschi Rue)

Below: This hybrid buck is the result of a white-tailed buck that bred a black-tailed doe. (Photograph by Leonard Lee Rue III)

White-tailed Deer

Range: The white-tailed deer (*Odocoileus virginianus*) is the most adaptable deer in the world, having the largest range and living under the most diverse conditions. It is also the oldest deer, having evolved about 3 million years ago.

The thirty-eight subspecies are found from the tropical forests of Central and South America to the edge of the boreal forests in Canada. I have seen them as far north as the Coal River, just a few miles south of Canada's Northwest Territories. They are found in every type of habitat in that vast area, from islands to mountains, in marshes and swamps, and on the plains. They are equally at home in jungles, grasslands, and forests, in wilderness areas, and in suburban and urban areas. They thrive on most agricultural lands.

Description: The various subspecies of white-tailed deer differ widely in body size, weight, and antler development, with the northern subspecies being much larger than their tropical counterparts. The gender dimorphism between male and female is much more disparate in northern subspecies than it is in the tropics, where the sexes are almost the same size.

Taking into account the diversity of the subspecies, a whitetail measures between 33 and 81.9 inches (850 and 2,100 mm) in head and body length. Tail length also varies greatly and can measure between 3.9 and 13.6 inches (100 and 350 mm). The deer may stand 21.4 to 42.9 inches (550 to 1,100 mm) high at the shoulder, and weigh between 39.6 and 473 pounds (18 and 215 kg). The record weights belong to two whitetail bucks in Minnesota that each weighed 510 pounds (232 kg).

The whitetail is probably our best known, most studied, most controversial, best loved, most sought after, and most disliked species in North America. It all depends upon your viewpoint. (Photograph by Uschi Rue)

Map of white-tailed deer range in the Americas

In North America the deer subspecies have two annual coats of hair. In the tropics they do not. The summer coat of the northern deer is usually a bright russet-red on the head, neck, and body. The belly, the inside of the legs, a throat patch, and the underside of the tail are pure white. The summer hair is thin, short, and solid; there are about 5,200 summer hairs to the square inch. The hair is primarily for insect protection, although it is also water repellent and helps to deflect the sun's rays, allowing the deer to be cooler. The winter coat of hair has about 2,600 guard hairs to the square inch; the hairs are long, hollow, kinky, and filled with air, providing excellent insulation. The deer have a short, woolly undercoat in the winter for additional warmth. The winter coat's color can range from different shades of tan to dark brown to almost dark gray. The winter coat is maintained from mid-August to mid-May, by which time it has bleached much lighter than its original color. The summer coat is worn only from mid-May to mid-August.

The white-tailed deer is so named because the undersurface of the tail is pure white. When the deer is excited, the tail is fully erected and the long hairs can be flared out as much as 11 inches (279 mm). The upper tail surface is usually brown, but the hairs may also be partially or all black.

The whitetail has forehead, preorbital, nasal, salivary, preputial, tarsal, metatarsal, and interdigital scent glands. The pedicles are about .75 inch (19 mm) in length and take about six months to fully develop. The pedicles and the antler's base grow larger each year of the deer's life. The antlers themselves may grow larger or be smaller in succeeding years, depending upon the available food in that particular year. Many white-tailed bucks grow a set of spike antlers when they are yearlings, caused by lack of protein in a buck's diet. If a whitetail has at least a 16 percent protein diet, its first set of antlers will have at least six points and perhaps eight.

Whitetail bucks do not mature until they are four years old. Prior to that time, the nutrients in the food they eat goes first to daily body maintenance and then to body growth. After bucks mature and the demands of maintenance have been met, the extra nutrition can be directed to their antlers. That's why the largest antlers are always found on mature animals, if they have access to nutritious food. Antlers continue to get larger until a buck is about nine years old. Then they begin to regress in size as the buck's teeth wear out and he cannot masticate his food thoroughly enough to get nutrients into his body.

Ordinarily, whitetail does do not have antlers. Research has shown that about one out of 4,000 does has enough testosterone in her system to grow antlers, but not enough to cause her antlers to harden. The soft antlers usually freeze off. (Such does are still capable of bearing and nursing young.)

Generally, white-tailed deer do not have canine teeth in the upper jaw, although rudimentary teeth are occasionally found. In New York state, less than 0.1 percent of deer have them. In the southern United States as many as 4.2 percent of deer possess rudimentary canine teeth. The farther south you go, the more common they are. In Venezuela, as many as 40 percent of white-tailed deer have rudimentary canine teeth.

Habits: White-tailed deer are selective feeders in that they carefully pick out particular plants to eat. By choice they are browsing animals but, because of their large population, they often completely destroy their preferred foods. In most cases, where such diversity is possible, the deer are known to eat as many as 650 types of vegetation. Browse, such as leaves, buds, and tips of twigs; mast crops, such as acorns, beechnuts, and hickory nuts; fruits; berries; mushrooms; forbs; grasses; and most farm crops are all readily eaten.

Whitetails have a basic matriarchal society made up of groups of blood-related females and their young, and led by the oldest doe. Such a grouping usually comprises three generations and, rarely, four.

White-tailed deer are not territorial, but they do have home ranges of 1 to 2 square miles (259 to 518 ha), depending on the amount of food and water available. It is only just prior to, during, and immediately after the birthing period that each adult doe will claim an individual territory away from the group. This act scatters the deer over the largest area possible to reduce predation and prevent newborn fawns from imprinting on other does.

Bucks form social groups of usually three to four individuals and sometimes as many as eight. The

The Florida Key deer is the smallest subspecies of white-tailed deer found in the United States. (Photograph by Uschi Rue)

The thick, insulating coat of hair allows this white-tailed buck to withstand winter's snow and cold. (Photograph by Uschi Rue)

bucks bond by frequent social grooming. A great deal of sparring takes place, as the bucks constantly test each other's strength. Starting as early as two weeks of age, this testing determines the social standing, or rank, of each deer. Only the top ranked, or dominant, bucks get to breed.

Whitetails usually walk slowly and cautiously from place to place, taking a bite of food here and there. They walk at a speed of 3 to 4 miles per hour (5 to 6 kmh); they trot at speeds of 6 to 8 miles per hour (10 to 13 kmh); and they have been clocked at a top speed of up to 45 miles per hour (72 kmh). I personally have seen them jump from a standing position over a 9.5-foot (3 m) high fence.

White-tailed deer are most active from just before dawn until about 8 A.M., and again from dusk until just after night falls. They actually are active again between 11 A.M. and noon, but as they only move about in their bedding area, they are seldom seen. They are also active between 10 and 11 P.M. and 2 and 3 A.M., but such activity is not generally observed because of darkness. They spend between 60 and 70 percent of their time lying in some safe place chewing their cud. If there are any hills in their area, the deer will usually bed down on the top of them during the daytime, so that the scent of any danger below is carried up to them on the rising thermals. In the evening, as the earth cools, the thermals reverse themselves and the air currents push down to the valley. At night the deer usually bed in their feeding areas. In cold weather, they will bed on the south side of hills to take advantage of whatever warmth the sun might have. They will also feed later in the morning and earlier in the afternoon in very cold weather. In summertime, they move to the north side of hilltops, in order to stay cool.

The northern members of all of the deer families, including whitetails, have a gradual slowing down of their basic body metabolism in the winter. As the temperature drops in late November, the deer become less active and their basic food requirements are cut as much as 60 percent. Their bodies need less food at the very time of the year that food becomes scarce, and the food that is available has less nutritional value than it has in warm weather.

Northern deer, because of strong winds and snow depth, may migrate to low-lying areas that have heavy cover to protect them from the elements. In these "deer yards," the conifers hold a lot of the snow load aloft in the branches and break the force of the wind. Because many of these yards are traditional and have been used forever, food may be scarce there, but the network of trails the deer make and the protection from the elements is more important than the availability of food. As long as the deer remain yarded, their caloric expenditure is low and they can survive as long as sixty days without food if they entered the yard in good shape. White-tailed deer in warmer climes may be forced to shift their home range in response to food and water, but they have an aversion to leaving their home range. The intimate knowledge of their range—every food source, water supply, trail, and hiding spot—is their main defense against all adversity.

Communication: Whitetails communicate with each other primarily through body language. A head held high denotes anxiety and instantly lets every other deer know that there might be danger. The higher the head is held, the greater the anxiety.

If a buck approaches another with his head held high, it is a sign of dominance. The subordinate deer will lower his head and avert his eyes, and perhaps even start to feed. A lowered head with the chin tucked in, the antlers projected forward, the ears swept back, and all the body hair raised on end is a posture of extreme aggression. If done as a challenge, the buck will approach in a sidling position with his head tilted slightly away from his rival—a position known as the "hard stare." The buck looks larger than usual because all the body hair is standing on end, and he appears much darker in color, because you are looking into the hairs.

One of the best known visual signals of the white-tailed deer is "flagging." When deer become alert or frightened, they raise their tails to a vertical position and flare the hairs. Deer are also capable of erecting the white hair on their rump and turning the hairs outward in a rosette. This show of white hair can be seen for a long distance. When does run off, they raise their tails, flair the hair, and allow the tail to flop loosely from side to side. It is this beacon that fawns follow as they dash after their mothers through dark forests. Although bucks are often depicted as running off with their tail raised, more often they clamp their tail down so as not to call attention to their departure.

When bucks rub off the dark outer bark of saplings, exposing the white inner wood, they are making a visual signal that lasts for months, until the white wood is darkened by the elements.

Whitetails have a large repertoire of vocal signals. The best known is the snort that signals danger to every deer that hears it. The deer also give a higher-pitched whistling snort, called the sneeze-snort, which means "extreme danger" and galvanizes every deer into instant retreat. Bucks make a low-pitched grunt when they are tracking an estrus doe. They make a low-pitched raspy grunt when they are challenging another buck or when they are frustrated. Does make a high grunt when talking to their fawns, and a soft bleating or "mooing" when they are searching for their fawns. Fawns make a loud bleating call when they are frightened, and a low murmuring sound while nursing.

Whitetails frequently stamp their feet when they are nervous, and that signal can be seen, heard, smelled, and felt through the ground.

Living in a world of scent, deer make efficient chemical signposts using odors from their various glands, urine, and feces. The advantage of the chemical signposts is that individual deer do not have to see each other to communicate. Signposts may last for hours, days, and even weeks until the scent is dissipated by the elements.

In making rubs, bucks are not only removing the bark of the tree, they are depositing scent from their forehead, preorbital, nasal, and salivary glands on the wood. DNA studies have proven that a deer's various scents are as individual as human fingerprints. The white-tailed bucks also frequently stand on their hind feet and mark high overhead branches with scent, "preaching" in the same fashion as chital and sambar stags.

Just prior to the rut, bucks make scrapes. Almost all scrapes are made under an overhanging branch, which the buck chews on to crush the twigs so they will hold more saliva. He hooks the branch with his antlers and deposits forehead and preorbital scent on

it. On the ground, he then uses his hooves to scrape a circular depression about 30 inches (762 mm) across. In so doing, he deposits scent from the interdigital gland between his hooves. He then puts his hind feet together, rubs his tarsal glands against each other, and urinates; the urine carries his tarsal gland scent down his legs to the ground.

Breeding: With the shortening of daylight hours after June 22, and in response to photoperiodism, testosterone levels rise in the white-tailed buck, setting in process the hardening of antlers, the peeling of the velvet, and the preparation for the rut. In northern deer this act takes place in August and September. In the southern United States it occurs in November and December, and in the tropics it can occur any time of the year. Although bucks are capable of breeding soon after their antlers are cleaned of velvet, no does are capable of accepting them for about another two months.

The actual rut lasts about two months. During that time, bucks' necks are greatly swollen from increased muscle use and the retention of more fluid in the cells, which acts a shock absorber. Does are estrus for a period of twenty-eight to thirty hours. If a doe is not bred or does not conceive during that period, she will recycle every twenty-eight days for as many as seven to eight times.

About forty-eight hours before the doe has her estrus period, she becomes exceptionally high-strung and begins to actively seek out a dominant buck. She trickles a trail of urine containing the pheromones announcing her pre-estrus condition, a trail every buck will instantly follow. The dominant buck will patrol a circle of about 150 feet (45 m), trying to keep the doe in the center and all other bucks out. It is an exceedingly hectic time, with constant chases, occasional fights, and with the doe being bred about once every four hours.

The adult buck will court the doe by caressing her with his body and licking her head and her vulva with his tongue. It is detrimental to a deer herd if there are no dominant bucks to maintain order during the breeding season. Young bucks lack courtship techniques and utilize a wilder chasing approach, so that all the animals lose weight and go into winter in

Genetics are important. This seven-month-old white-tailed button buck was probably sired by the big buck standing behind him. If he has access to sufficient nutritious food, with age his antlers should grow as large as his father's. (Photograph by Uschi Rue)

White-tailed bucks in bachelor groups often do social grooming. (Photograph by Leonard Lee Rue III)

poorer condition. Often non-estrus does will assemble within the dominant buck's protective circle so that young bucks are unable to follow them.

Birth and Young: The gestation period for white-tailed doe varies between 195 and 203 days; the shorter time is attained by the best-fed does. In areas that have highly nutritious food, 60 to 80 percent of female fawns will achieve a weight of around 80 pounds (30 kg) and will breed when they are seven months old; all others breed at seventeen to eighteen months.

Does giving birth for the first time usually produce a singleton; thereafter twins are the norm. In areas with highly nutritious food, does often give birth to triplets and occasionally quadruplets.

Just prior to giving birth, a doe will establish a birthing territory and drive off all other deer, including her previous year's fawns. At this time some young bucks may disperse permanently. Within three weeks, young does rejoin their mother and her new fawns. Young bucks that also rejoin the doe will be driven off permanently at about fifteen to sixteen months of age. This act prevents familial interbreeding and thus strengthens the gene pool.

Newborn fawns average between 6 and 8 pounds (3 to 4 kg) at birth. Fawns weighing less than 5 pounds (2 kg) do not have a good chance of survival. Mortality for fawns from all causes runs as high as 40 percent. On their mother's rich milk, which has a butter-fat content of 11 to 12 percent, fawns grow rapidly. They have a spotted coat and remain hidden for the first two to three weeks of life. Thereafter they follow after their mothers.

Fawns' spotted coats are lost at about four months of age. In the north, fawns stop growing at about six months of age, as fat accumulation takes precedence over skeletal growth. At this time they are about two-thirds the size of does.

The average lifespan of a white-tailed deer is about twelve years, but both wild and captive deer have lived to be twenty-three years old.

Enemies: It is a good thing that the annual recruitment rate for white-tailed deer on good habitat is about 40 percent per year. The deer are preyed upon by cougars, bears, wolves, coyote, bobcats, and dogs. Even foxes occasionally take fawns.

Whitetails are plagued by diseases and parasites. Hard winters exact a tremendous toll on the northern deer and losses can run into the hundreds of thousands of animals. In many areas, the deer is its own worst enemy because large populations rapidly decimate their own habitat.

Relationship with Humans: The white-tailed deer is the most important big game animal in North America. Over 6,250,000 deer are harvested every year, more than any other large animal anywhere in the world. To protect this valuable resource, the white-tailed deer has become the most managed wild animal in the world.

The ax and the plow decimated many species, but allowed white-tailed deer to increase its population to an estimated 30 million animals in the United States alone. Their consumption, and often destruction, of farm crops, gardens, orchards, and ornamental shrubs make them disliked by farmers, gardeners, and suburban homeowners.

Motorists fear whitetails, as the deer cause over 500,000 accidents a year, resulting in more than 200,000 injuries, more than 200 human deaths, and a loss of more than a billion dollars in damage. Most accidents occur between 2 and 3 A.M. in the months of May, June, October, and November. This higher incidence of accidents is caused by the dispersal of the yearlings in spring and by rutting season in the fall.

Above: White-tailed bucks have the large haunches needed for saltatorial bounding. (Photograph by Leonard Lee Rue III)

Right: A white-tailed buck has been recorded jumping 29 feet (9 m) horizontally and 9.5 feet (2.9 m) vertically, and running at a top speed of 45 miles per hour (73 kph). (Photograph by Len Rue Jr.)

A group of white-tailed bucks feeds in the early morning fog. (Photograph by Uschi Rue)

By laying his ears back and erecting his body hair, this white-tailed buck is using body language to show his aggression. (Photograph by Uschi Rue)

If white-tailed bucks cannot intimidate their rivals using body language, they will have to fight to determine dominance. (Photograph by Leonard Lee Rue III)

The blood and hair on this white-tailed buck's antlers show that he severely wounded his opponent in a fight. (Photograph by Leonard Lee Rue III)

Right: Some white-tailed bucks run off with their tails up, but most keep their tails clamped down so as not to attract the attention of the predator. (Photograph by Leonard Lee Rue III)

Below: By vigorously rubbing a sapling, the white-tailed buck is not only making a visual and olfactory signpost, he is also strengthening his body before the battles of rutting season begin. (Photograph by Uschi Rue)

Above: The greatly swollen neck on this white-tailed buck denotes that rutting season is in full swing. (Photograph by Uschi Rue)

Left: Cougars, the largest cats in North America, prey heavily upon both mule and white-tailed deer. When it has eaten its fill, this cougar will cover with leaves and other debris the remains of the white-tailed deer carcass. (Photograph by Leonard Lee Rue III)

Right: White-tailed does keep their fawns hidden for the first two to three weeks of their life, coming back to nurse them three or four times in a twenty-four-hour period. (Photograph by Leonard Lee Rue III)

Below: At each nursing period, the white-tailed doe washes her fawns and consumes their urine and feces to prevent leaving any odor that might attract a predator. (Photograph by Leonard Lee Rue III)

Left: White-tailed fawns are a "hider" species, depending upon immobility and cryptic coloration to escape detection. (Photograph by Len Rue Jr.)

Below: At just five days of age, a white-tailed fawn can outrun a person. (Photograph by Len Rue Jr.)

Marsh Deer

Range: The marsh deer (*Blastocerus dichotomus*) is found in southwestern Brazil, Paraguay, and the northern tip of Uruguay and Argentina.

Description: The marsh deer is the largest deer in South America, with a head and body length of 59.6 to 76 inches (1,530 to 1,950 mm) and a tail length of 3.9 to 6.2 inches (100 to 160 mm). It stands 42.9 to 49.5 inches (1,100 to 1,270 mm) at the shoulder, and weighs between 176 and 330 pounds (80 and 150 kg).

Marsh deer have a bright russet-red summer coat and a reddish-brown winter coat. The hair of both coats is long and coarse. These deer have a black band across their nose, and the lower two-thirds of their long legs are black. They have large ears that are white on the inside. Their tail is rusty-yellow on the undersurface and all black on top. When marsh deer run off, they erect their tails vertically, as do white-tailed deer.

Marsh deer have prominent preorbital glands, as well as tarsal, interdigital, and nasal glands. Their feet are unique in that they have a web-like membrane between the two long center hooves. The membrane greatly increases the bearing surface of each foot and keeps the deer from sinking when they walk in mud. Their dewclaws are long enough to reach the ground, giving additional support. Marsh deer have no maxillary canine teeth.

The brow tine of the marsh deer's antlers is bifurcated. The main beam sweeps back then forward with four to six tines or points pointing to the rear. Marsh deer are not governed by photoperiodism and so their antler growth, rutting season, and birthing period may occur at any time of the year.

Habits: These deer, as their name implies, live in marshlands and swamps. The annual floods that occur in their areas often restrict their range and force them to seek high ground. Marsh deer are hiders and

The marsh deer is the largest deer found in either South or North America, with some of the biggest bucks standing 49 inches (1,245 mm) high at the shoulder. (Photograph © Heather Angel/Natural Visions)

conceal themselves in amongst high reeds in the hope they will not be discovered. When they are pushed from cover, they use a saltatorial gait, bounding away like an oversized jackrabbit. This gait is the most efficient means of running in water, which may be 2 feet (610 mm) deep in their habitat.

Marsh deer feed upon grasses, reeds, rushes, and emergent vegetation.

Communication: Very little is known about the communication methods of these deer. There is no record of their vocalizations, although they undoubtedly rub the scent from their preorbital glands on bushes.

Breeding: Because these deer can breed at any time of the year, the individual bucks and does reach their breeding potential at different times of the year. Therefore, dominance among bucks is not as important as it is among other species of deer. Little sparring is done among young males, and almost no fighting is done by adult bucks. Bucks do not gather harems, but seek out estrus does as each comes into her individual cycle.

Birth and Young: The gestation period for marsh deer is a long one, lasting 255 to 271 days. The doe gives birth to a singleton, which has an unspotted coat.

This unspotted coat is most unusual for an animal that depends upon hiding. Fawns, which weigh about 9.2 pounds (4 kg), are comparatively small given the size of the adult animals. This small birth weight and the long gestation period indicate that the food these animals eat is low in nutrition. Does are subject to postpartum estrus and breed again within days of giving birth. The young of both sexes do not mature until they are two years old.

Enemies: Marsh deer have few natural enemies, but the maned wolf, jaguar, cougar, and the giant anaconda snake are the main enemies.

Relationship with Humans: The marsh deer is an endangered species because of over-hunting, the conversion of its habitat for agriculture, competition from imported foreign deer species, and the spread of disease from domestic cattle.

Pampas Deer

Range: The pampas deer (*Ozotocerus bezoarticus*) is a grassland dweller that is found in Brazil, Bolivia, Paraguay, Uruguay, and northern Argentina. It is equally at home along flooded riverine bottoms and on low, dry, rolling hills.

Description: This is a small deer, with a head and body length of 42.9 to 54.6 inches (1,100 to 1,400 mm) and a tail length of 3.9 to 5.8 inches (100 to 150 mm). There is almost no dimorphism between the sexes; both male and female stand between 27.3 and 29.2 inches (693 to 742 mm) high at the shoulder, and weigh between 55 and 88 pounds (25 and 40 kg).

The pampas deer is nicknamed "the stinking deer" because the strong onion odor of its interdigital glands can be smelled at a considerable distance. Even its meat has this strong odor and so is not often used by humans for food. This species also has prominent preorbital, nasal, and tarsal glands.

These deer have a basic, uniform, light tan to brown coloration with a slightly lighter color on the belly and the inside of the legs. Winter and summer coats are the same color. The underside of the tail and the rump patches are white, and the hair on both can be flared. These deer erect their tails vertically when they run.

The antlers of the pampas deer are basically three tined with a forward projecting brow tine and a bifurcated main beam. A good buck's antlers may measure up to 13.5 inches (340 mm). The antlers are usually cast in August. There are small whorls of hair on the doe's head where the bucks have antlers.

Habits: Although it is an animal of vast, treeless plains, the pampas deer usually prefers to be in high grass that offers good protective cover. When threatened, it hides among the grasses to escape detection and will run off only if it must. As hiders, these deer are usually solitary or found in small family groups of no more than five to six animals. Larger herds may form in areas where new grass is sprouting or in areas that have browse. Pampas deer are known to occasionally feed under cover of darkness, but most feeding is done in the early morning and late afternoon. They feed mainly upon grasses and forbs, but they also eat reeds and rushes along river bottoms. Pampas deer often stand on their hind legs to reach the browse of high growing bushes and to be able to look over the top of the high grasses in which they live.

Communication: Pampas deer use their preorbital glands to mark their scent on vegetation; they also flare their glands to send the scent out on the air currents. During rutting season, bucks make scrapes by pawing vigorously with their forefeet, then deposit urine on the exposed earth. Occasionally they also defecate in the scrapes. When they hook bushes with their antlers, they leave visual signs as well as scent.

During the rut, bucks make a low, buzzy, raspy call, which is quite similar to the bleat made by fawns. The bleat of the doe is of a higher pitch.

When pampas deer are alarmed, they give a whistling snort and stamp their forefeet in way similar to that of white-tailed deer. They will then either sneak or dash off with their white tails prominently showing.

Breeding: Pampas deer do not defend territories nor do they try to gather harems during rutting season, which occurs in January and February. Bucks simply roam among female groups, searching for estrus does. Sparring is common among males, and they use both body language and redirected aggression, such as thrashing bushes, to prove their dominance. Fights

As its name implies, the pampas deer lives on the rolling grasslands of central South America. (Photograph © Erwin & Peggy Bauer)

between two dominant males are quite common. What is uncommon is that bucks sometimes bite their rivals.

The courtship pattern of pampas deer is similar to that of white-tailed deer, wherein the buck will approach a pre-estrus female with his head held low and outstretched. The buck will nuzzle the doe and lick her body and vulva to stimulate her. The female, if not quite ready to breed, will lead the male on a long chase until she is ready to stand. At times, to avoid harassment, the female will lie flat on the ground; at other times she will constantly keep turning away.

Birth and Young: The gestation period for pampas deer is between 210 and 215 days. When the doe is about to give birth, she goes off by herself to an area that provides protective cover. Only a single, spotted fawn is born. It will weigh about 4.8 pounds (2 kg).

The doe will keep her fawn away from the herd for at least two weeks so that the fawn imprints on only her and will not follow after any other doe. The fawn begins to eat various types of vegetation before it follows after its mother. It is usually weaned by three months, loses it spots at four months, and stays with its mother until it is about one year old.

In captivity, a pampas deer lived to be twenty-one years, one month old.

Enemies: Because of its environment, the pampas deer does not have many natural enemies. It is preyed upon by the maned wolf and occasionally the cougar.

Relationship with Humans: The pampas deer is on the endangered species list because of the exploitation of its range by cattlemen and the diseases of livestock. Pampas deer also give way before the competition of imported species, such as red deer and wapiti.

Huemuls

Range: There are two species of the huemul or Andean deer—the northern or Peruvian huemul (*Hippocamelus antisensis*) and the southern or Chilean huemul (*Hippocamelus bisulcus*). In some literature these deer are also referred to as *guemels* or, for the northern species, by their Spanish name of *taruka*. They are found in the Andes Mountains in Ecuador, Peru, Brazil, Bolivia, Chile, and Argentina. They are high mountain deer and are seldom found below 13,000 feet (3,960 m). The two species are kept separate by a desert area along the Argentina-Chile border.

Description: There is considerable size difference between the huemul found in the southern Andes and the taruka found in more northern countries. This size difference is the result of Bergmann's Rule, which states that animals farther from the equator will be larger than those that are close to it.

The two species average between 54.6 and 64.3 inches (1,400 and 1,650 mm) in head and body length, with a tail measuring 1.1 to 4.4 inches (30 to 115 mm). Males stand between 30.2 and 35.1 inches (775 and 900 mm) high at the shoulder, and weigh between 99 and 143 pounds (45 and 65 kg). Females are 25 to 30 percent smaller in stature and weight than males.

Huemuls have a stocky body on short, sturdy legs. Their hooves have a slope of only about 75 degrees. These straight hooves allow them to scramble around on rocky ledges with the agility of wild sheep. The outer hoof is hard with a spongy center that protrudes just slightly beyond the hard hoof and allows for good purchase on slippery rocks.

Both sexes of both species have rudimentary canine teeth that seldom break through the gum line. They have large preorbital and tarsal glands, but lack metatarsals.

The huemul's hair is long and coarse, and it is longest on the head and tail. The basic body colora-

The Peruvian huemul inhabits the mountainous regions of the Andes Mountains. The bucks have just two-tined antlers. (Photograph © Andres Morya)

Map of huemul range in South America

Northern/Peruvian huemul
(*Hippocamelus antisensis*)

Southern/Chilean huemul
(*Hippocamelus bisulcus*)

tion is reddish-brown. The ears are long and narrow, which is unusual in a mountain animal that depends more on its eyesight than on auditory stimulation. The inside of the ears are white. The huemel has an indistinct eyering and a white band that goes entirely around the muzzle. The inside of the legs are a dirty white and there are patches of white on each flank. The undertail surface is white on the taruka, while that of the southern huemul has a brown under-surface.

The antlers of the huemuls have a single crotch, or fork, on each side of the head with the anterior tines being the shorter of the two. The longest tines seldom measure more than 11 inches (280 mm). Antlers may be cast at different times of the year for the taruka, but the southern huemul usually casts its antlers in September or October.

Habits: These animals live in high mountain meadows during summer, then drop down to lower elevations, even going into forests when the snows begin to deepen.

Huemuls have an unusual habit for deer in that they remain paired throughout the year. They seldom herd, and the small groupings of six to eight animals that are sometimes seen are blood-related family groups of up to three generations. Bucks do not form bachelor groups.

The lack of herding is indicative of poor forage conditions with sparse vegetation that is coarse and low in nutrition. Huemuls feed primarily on grasses, sedges, and forbs. When they are forced down to the forested areas, they browse on twig tips. With the vegetation low in nutrition, huemuls have to process more food than is normal for most species, which means they spend longer periods feeding than do other types of deer. Feeding is usually done during daylight hours because huemuls, like wild sheep, don't move about much at night.

The huemul depends upon the ability to hide to escape detection. As soon as possible after being discovered, a huemul will usually attempt to steal away and seek out another hiding spot. It is neither a fast nor a long distance runner. However, if pushed from its hiding place, it will dash off, all the while attempting to put some obstacle between itself and its discoverer.

Communication: Bucks make a soft, rapid call that has been described as a laugh. The duration of this call is short and can only be heard if the deer is close. Fawns have a high-pitched bleat.

Huemul bucks thrash bushes with their antlers, exposing the white inner bark, and then deposit scent from their preorbital glands thereon. Bucks also use their antlers to tear up the ground and then wear the grass on their antlers like a crown. They have also been observed lying down in spots in which they had just urinated, creating wallows.

Breeding: There is a great deal of sparring among huemul bucks, but real fighting is rare. Ordinarily, lesser bucks initiate sparring with dominant bucks. Despite the fact that these deer are paired up all year, the pairs also engage in considerable courtship chasing. Bucks court their estrus does with body and vulva licking.

Birth and Young: Huemuls have a long gestation period of about 240 days—another indication of the low nutritional value of the vegetation they eat. One and sometimes two unspotted fawns are born in the months of late February to April. Fawns weigh between 5 and 6 pounds (2 and 3 kg). Prior to giving birth, the doe chases off her previous year's young, and retires to some secluded spot of safety. She stays apart from her fawn, coming back to nurse it about four times a day. When the fawn is between three and four weeks of age, the doe allows it to follow her as she rejoins the buck. Fawns stay with does until does are ready to give birth again the following year.

In captivity, a huemul lived to be ten years, nine months old. I am sure that they can live to be close to twenty years, because large animals live longer than small ones, but I can find no records to substantiate this.

Enemies: The cougar is the huemul's main enemy, although both domestic and feral dogs also take a toll.

Relationship with Humans: The destruction of habitat by farmers, ranchers, and lumbermen have caused the populations of both species of huemul to drop to the point that they are now considered endangered.

Brocket Deer

Range: The four species of brockets—red (*Mazama americana*), brown (*Mazama gouazoubira*), little red (*Mazama rufina*), and dwarf (*Mazama chunyi*)—are found from central Mexico south to northern Argentina. They are found from sea level up to altitudes of 12,500 feet (3,800 m).

Description: As their names indicate, the four species vary in size, weight, and color. Brockets average from 28 to 52.6 inches (720 to 1,350 mm) in head and body length, with a tail length from 1.9 to 7.8 inches (48 to 200 mm). They stand 13.6 to 29.2 inches (350 to 750 mm) high at the shoulder, and weigh between 17.6 and 55 pounds (8 to 24 kg). Some exceptional bucks from Suriname have weighed as much as 143 pounds (65 kg).

The hair on brockets is long and coarse, with the longest hair found on the head and tail. There are two whorls of hair on the foreheads of both sexes. Basic body coloration varies from light tannish-red to deep russet-red. All species have lighter-colored underparts and inner legs. The underside of the tail is white.

Brocket deer's bodies are stocky, but their legs are slim and comparatively short, although not as short as those of the pudu. Their size and shape is an adaptation to being a hider species that inhabits dense, brushy cover. Their backs arch, giving them a slightly humped appearance.

Brockets have deciduous canine teeth that, when lost, grow back as permanent incisors in only about 20 percent of the animals. Their antlers are straight, short spikes growing no more than 3.5 to 5 inches (88 to 127 mm) in length. The antlers rarely develop tines. As tropical animals, brocket bucks have neither a set time for antler growth to start, nor a set time for antlers to be cast. Research indicates that some bucks may actually retain their hardened antlers for more than a year. Brockets have both forehead and preorbital scent glands.

Habits: As inhabitants of dense cover, brockets are not built for speed. If possible, they remain hidden to escape detection. When discovered, they bound away in a saltatorial gait, trying to put obstructions between themselves and their pursuers. Whenever possible, they take to water to escape danger, as they are strong swimmers.

Brockets are basically solitary and, as such, have personal territories they defend against rivals. Male brockets have much larger territories than do females, and each male's territory often overlaps that of two to three females' territories.

Brockets are browsers, feeding on the tender new shoots of shrubs, bushes, and vines. They eat grasses and both freshly fallen and dried fruits and berries. Mushrooms make up a large part of the brocket's diet and can be found the year round in the tropics. Brockets also eat some emergent water plants.

Researchers have found that brockets, like white-tailed deer, are active at night, although the bulk of feeding is done in early morning and late afternoon.

Communication: Brocket bucks frequently rub bushes and saplings with their antlers, exposing the white inner bark as a visual sign. They then rub scent from both their forehead and preorbital glands on the exposed wood, leaving their individualized olfactory "no trespassing" sign.

When alarmed, these deer stamp their feet, sending a signal that is seen, heard, and felt by cohorts and predators. Brockets also erect their tails, showing the white undersurface, to flash their alarm.

Researchers write of the brocket making a piercing call. Because they share so many other characteristics of the white-tailed deer, they probably snort, grunt, and bleat also.

Breeding: Because they are tropical, these deer are not governed by photoperiodism and have no set breeding season. When does are pre-estrus, they seek out males. A doe leaves a trail of dribbled urine containing the pheromones that guarantee that any male finding her trail is sure to follow her. She may run from bucks until she is sufficiently stimulated to stand.

Dominant males drive off lesser males with body language. When two equal males follow after the same female, breeding rights go to the strongest and best. When brocket bucks fight, they often rear up on their hind feet, like goats and sheep, and then drop down to bang their heads together. They will also occasionally jump over their rival. Most actual fighting is done

Red brocket deer are usually found in the densely forested regions of Mexico. (Photograph by Len Rue Jr.)

in a side-by-side position, with each buck standing head to tail to the other. The bucks then swing their heads up from a low position to try to slash their rival's body. Wild goats, which fight in a similar position, have thick hide on their flanks as a protection against the upward stabbing horns of their rivals. Researchers do not mention that brockets have a similarly thick hide on their flanks, but the fact that they fight in this manner indicates that their hides should be thicker there. When fighting, brockets also attempt to bite each other, though they have no front teeth in their top jaw.

Birth and Young: The gestation period for brockets is about 230 to 240 days. While some species give birth to a singleton, most have twins. As befits a hider species, fawns are spotted and kept hidden for the first three weeks of life. The young, when born, weigh between 1.2 and 5 pounds (.6 and 2 kg), according to the species. Brockets mature rapidly, and females may be capable of breeding before they are one year old.

In captivity, a brocket lived to be sixteen years old.

Enemies: Brockets have many enemies, including cougars, jaguars, anacondas, farmers' dogs, and other meat eaters.

Relationship with Humans: Brockets are a threatened species because their habitat is being converted for farming purposes. They are shot for food and as nuisance animals, because they often feed upon crops. Unless they are given more protection, their future as a species is not bright.

Pudu

Range: There are two species of pudu. *Pudu pudu* ranges on the western foothills of the Andes Mountains in Chile and Argentina at elevations from sea level up to 5,577 feet (1,700 m). *Pudu mephistophiles* is found in Colombia, Ecuador, and Peru, living at elevations up to 13,124 feet (4,000 m).

Description: The pudu are the smallest deer in the world. They average between 23.4 and 32.1 inches (600 and 825 mm) in body length. Their tail is almost non-existent, less than 1 inch (25 mm) long. Pudu stand between 9.75 and 16.7 inches (250 and 430 mm) high at the shoulder, and weigh between 12.7 and 29.4 pounds (6 and 13 kg). The sexes are approximately the same size. As a species, the southern pudu is smaller than its northern counterpart.

Pudu are similar in appearance to the little forest Duiker antelope of Africa. Pudu have a stocky body with a humped back at the hips, and short, thin legs with dainty hooves. Inhabiting heavily forested regions and hiders by nature, pudu do not need to hear danger approaching at a great distance. Consequently, their ears are short and well rounded.

The antlers of the males are simple spikes, measuring 3 to 4 inches (76 to 102 mm). The antlers do not appear to be that long, because their bases are hidden in a roach of stiff hairs growing on the frontal skull of the animal. Pudu's antlers usually curve slightly backward.

Their eyes are small and their noses are slightly bulbous. Deciduous canine teeth are occasionally found. Pudu have large, prominent preorbital glands, which they flare open when excited. They do not have the tarsal or metatarsal glands so prominent on other species of deer.

Pudu's summer coats are various shades of reddish-brown; their winter coats are more grayish. Southern pudu, which live at lower elevations and in darker forests, are darker in coloration than their northern relative. Their hair is dense and coarse.

Habits: Creatures like the pudu that inhabit dense vegetation usually live solitary lives and defend the territory in which they live. Pudu depend upon hiding to escape enemies, and it's easier for a single animal to hide than for a group to hide. As hiders, pudu are stealthy, and sneak about among the vegetation, pausing frequently to look around and test the air for the scent of possible danger, before moving on again.

Because the vegetation is dense, a pudu lays out a network of trails throughout its claimed territory. The pudu's territory will vary in size from 40 to 64 acres

The southern pudu is the smallest deer in the world, with a buck standing about 10 inches (254 mm) high at the shoulder. (Photograph © Heather Angel/Natural Visions)

(16 to 26 ha), according to the amount of food that is available. The pudu is not a fast runner; it is considered a saltatorial runner, and when threatened it bounds over the vegetation, using the vegetation to screen it from its pursuers. The pudu has a small territory, which it knows intimately, and will run in circles when pursued because it does not want to venture into an area it does not know, which would put it at a disadvantage.

Although pudu feed in the grasslands bordering their forest habitat, they are primarily browsing animals. They feed heavily upon the leaves, twigs, and buds of the forest vegetation. They also eat berries, fruits, mushrooms, acorns, and other mast crops. They are not adverse to eating cultivated crops when they have access to them.

Communication: Because they are basically solitary, pudu are not very vocal. The most commonly heard sounds are a hiss-like whistle or high-pitched snort.

Pudu make frequent use of chemical signposts. Throughout their territory, males will chew upon and mark vegetation with scent from their preorbital glands. They stop frequently along their trails, paw the ground, and then urinate and defecate in their scrapings. This act proclaims ownership of a particular area, and also saturates an entire area with the pudu's odor, making it much harder for a predator to pinpoint the pudu's exact location.

Breeding: Male pudu are basically solitary, but their territory overlaps that of several females and their young. Prior to and during rutting season, which occurs in March and April, little males vigorously hook small saplings and brush with their antlers and deposit scent from their preorbital and forehead glands on the exposed wood.

Male pudu are extremely aggressive in defending their territories and in fighting for the breeding rights to females. In addition to head-on charges so typical of most deer fighting, pudu also bite their opponents, although this is not very effective as they have lost their milk canine teeth by this age. These deer also fight standing upright and strike out at their adversaries with their hooves. In captivity, where several males are confined to one enclosure, pudu often fight so viciously that one of the combatants is killed.

During courtship, males approach a female with a low-crouched, low-head posture. Like the wapiti, the male pudu does a lot of tongue flicking and anal licking to stimulate the female.

Birth and Young: In November and December, the female gives birth to a single fawn after a gestation period of about 210 to 215 days. Fawns weigh less than 2 pounds (1 kg) at birth. An oddity is that fawns of northern pudu are spotted, while fawns of southern pudu are not. The young grow rapidly and have almost reached adult body size and weight in six months, at which time the little females are sexually mature. The little males' antlers begin to develop at three months of age, and harden and peel by the time they are one year old. At that time, they are also sexually mature.

Enemies: Dogs are pudu's major predator. When pursued by dogs, southern pudu often seek escape by taking to the water. The northern pudu is adept at scrambling over rocky terrain. Jaguars feed upon pudu, but are too scarce to take a heavy toll.

Relationship with Humans: Pudu are not plentiful in any area and are classified as a threatened species. The slash-and-burn agriculture practiced in South America, which results in the destruction of habitat, is causing the pudu population to decline precipitously.

Despite this fact, pudu are heavily hunted. The natives' need for protein, a lack of game laws, the improbability of enforcing laws that do exist, and year-round hunting and trapping all contribute to the steady decline in the pudu's population.

Moose

Range: Moose are creatures of the boreal, taiga, and tundra regions, and are found around the world in these habitats. I have found moose living on the tundra just 60 miles (96 km) south of the Arctic Ocean.

All moose today are classified as a single species, *Alces alces*. There is no argument against that classification, although experts differ widely on the number of subspecies. Whitehead lists six subspecies while Geist lists three. The North American moose is larger than that of Eurasia, and moose in both regions are larger in the northern regions than they are in the southern portions of their range. North American moose are today expanding their range farther south, despite the advent of global warming and the fact that they are cold-adapted creatures. Just a few years ago, a young bull moose wandered down into my home area of northwestern New Jersey, where moose have never before been documented.

Moose have tough, leathery lips so they can strip leaves from branches by pulling them through their mouths. (Photograph by Uschi Rue)

Description: The moose is the largest member of the deer family. There is a great sexual dimorphism in moose, with cows about 25 percent smaller in body size and up to 33.3 percent lighter in weight than bulls. Moose have a head and body length of 93.6 to 120.9 inches (2,400 to 3,100 mm) and a tail length of 1.9 to 4.2 inches (50 to 120 mm). They stand between 54.6 and 91.6 inches (1,400 and 2,350 mm) high at the shoulder and weigh between 400 and 1,815 pounds (200 and 825 kg).

In addition to their large size, bull moose are distinguished by their huge, palmated antlers. The Alaskan-Yukon moose, which is the largest subspecies and also has the largest antlers, often displays a double palmation of the antlers on each side of the head, known as the "butterfly pattern."

Another unique feature of the moose is the half-moon shaped flap of skin hanging below the throat, forming a dewlap or "bell." The bull's bell often has a pendulous rope of skin hanging down as much as 18 inches (457 mm). The cow lacks the dewlap flap of skin, but frequently has a rope. Some adult moose lack the rope because that skin sometimes freezes off.

A special adaptation of the moose is its wide overhanging muzzle. A bull's muzzle is black, while that of the cow is brown. Unlike most deer, which have bare muzzles, the moose's rhinarium is hair covered, except for about a 1-inch (25 mm) round spot in the center at the bottom of the upper lip. The moose has tough, leathery lips—and needs them, because when it feeds it frequently strips the leaves off branches by pulling the branches through its lips.

In coloration, the Eurasian moose has a uniform body color of light reddish-brown. American moose are reddish-brown on the upper half of their bodies, shading to almost black on their lower regions. The inner legs are tan, and there is a narrow black stripe running down the back from head to tail.

Both cows and bulls have a dark mane of long hair about 10 inches (254 mm) long on their neck and withers, with a crest of shorter hair over their rumps. When frightened or angry, moose erect these hairs. The erected mane is quickly followed by a lowering of the head and ears, then the tongue lolls out of its mouth, after which the moose will try to stomp on whatever is threatening it.

The dewclaws of the moose are long and help the splayed hooves provide more bearing surface and keep the animal from sinking in soft mud. The moose's long legs keep its belly about 40 inches (106 mm) off the ground, which is a tremendous advantage when walking in deep snow.

Moose do not have metatarsal glands, but do have small tarsal glands. They also have preorbital glands.

Map of moose range in North America

Map of moose range in Eurasia

Left: Bull moose often stay in small groups until rutting season causes them to be competitors. (Photograph by Leonard Lee Rue III)

Below: Alaska-Yukon bull moose have the largest antlers of any *Cervid* in the world. (Photograph by Leonard Lee Rue III)

Habits: Moose are basically solitary animals, except for cows with calves. Occasionally two or three bulls form a bachelor group, and in Alaska groups of ten to twelve animals may gather in traditional areas during breeding season. Deep snow may force moose to congregate in areas with less snow and ample food, but, basically, moose are loners.

I spent seventeen summers guiding canoe trips into virgin wilderness areas of Quebec when I was a young man. I saw moose almost every day, feeding on emergent and submerged vegetation in the ponds and lakes on which I canoed. These water plants are nutritious because nutrients and minerals from the entire region drain into the ponds and lakes. The water also gives moose relief from clouds of biting, blood-sucking flies and mosquitoes which curse the area.

I spent fourteen summers in Alaska and found many moose as high on the mountainsides as wild sheep. At higher elevations, a constant breeze gives moose relief from insect hoards that plague the lowlands. Moose are also safe there from grizzly bears, which kill most moose calves born in the willow brush bordering low-lying lakes and rivers.

In addition to browsing on the leaves and tender twig tips of brush and saplings, and on the water plants, moose eat many different types of reeds, grasses, sedges, berries, and fungi. In winter, when moose are feeding almost exclusively on browse, they often stand upright and straddle saplings with their forefeet. Using their chests, they allow their weight to bend or break the sapling so they can feed on the more nutritious top twigs. They also strip bark from the larger aspen, cottonwoods, willows, and birch trees using their lower incisor teeth as scrapers.

Although moose are loners, they do not control territories; instead, they have home ranges that are flexible. They do not migrate, but they do shift their ranges according to season, weather, and food availability.

It is absolutely amazing how an animal as large as a bull moose with huge antlers can move through a forest or brushland without making a sound, when it is being cautious. At other times, it crashes through the brush with all the subtlety of a bulldozer run amuck. Moose commonly just walk from place to place; if startled, they have a lumbering gallop. However, when a moose really wants to go somewhere in a hurry, it has a ground-eating trot it can keep up for miles. Moose have been clocked trotting at 37.2 miles

per hour (60 kmh). One observer talks of following a young cow moose on the road of Alaska's Kenai Peninsula for 6 miles (10 km). By clocking his car's speedometer, the driver knew the cow was trotting at 33 miles per hour (53 kmh). When he pushed her a little harder, she broke into a gallop and reached a speed of 45 miles per hour (72 kmh) without a great deal of effort.

Moose are strong swimmers. Their hollow hairs help to buoy them up, and their large hooves and great strength enable them to move swiftly through water.

Communication: The most common sound of the moose is a deep coughing grunt made by both cows and bulls, with the latter making deeper, raspier sounds. During rutting season, the cow gives a high-pitched, long, drawn-out squeal that carries for miles. Calves give a high-pitched bleat. Some folks describe moose calls as a wail, whine, bawl, or bellow.

Bulls thrash bushes and saplings, making visual signs and leaving their scent for olfactory signs. They also tear up soft turf with their antlers and forefeet, urinate copiously, and then wallow in the mud, coating their bell and body. The odor of a bull's urine is a strong sexual stimulant to cows.

Breeding: Rutting season for moose starts in mid-September and extends to the end of October. During this time, bulls become extremely aggressive and have been known to attack cars, bulldozers, and even trains.

Bulls employ body language to dominate rivals. They approach each other with their heads held high and the whites of their eyes showing. They rock their huge antlers from side to side as they walk with a stiff-legged gait. Lesser bulls quickly get out of the way; equal bulls may fight. The bulls crash together with tons of pressure as each tries to throw his rival off his feet and gore him. Occasionally the force of the initial impact will cause the bull's antlers to bend apart and then spring back, locking the two animals together. Unable to free themselves, both bulls will die of stress and starvation.

In some areas, the bull seeks out a single, estrus cow, and after breeding her, continues on his way, looking for another. In Alaska, bulls form harems of six to eight cows, with the dominant bull driving all other bulls away from his cows.

In summer, moose spend a lot of time feeding on both emergent and submerged water plants. (Photograph by Uschi Rue)

Birth and Young: The gestation period for moose varies between 240 and 246 days, with most calves born in May or June. Cow moose give birth to a singleton at their first birthing; thereafter, twins are the norm. A moose calf has a bright russet-red coat with no spots, and weighs between 25 and 45 pounds (11 and 16 kg). The cow keeps her calf hidden and stands guard nearby, attacking anything she considers a threat. A cow moose defending her calf is as dangerous as a she grizzly with cubs, and maybe more so. Within a few days after birth, the calf follows after the cow as she feeds, and is soon sampling the same vegetation the cow is eating. At the age of three months, the calf has been weaned and its coat has changed to dark brown. Calves stay with the cow until she chases them off in the spring, when she is ready to give birth to new calves. Young cows usually breed for the first time at fifteen months.

Enemies: The wolf is the moose's main predator, yet the moose that makes a determined stand can usually keep a pack at bay. Bull moose use their huge antlers for defense, but all moose can deliver powerful kicks both forward and backward, slashing their attacker with their large hooves. Grizzly bears take a tremendous toll on moose calves, as do black bears, though to a lesser extent.

Previously, many North American moose died as a result of being infected by the *Tenuis* brainworm, which they contracted from white-tailed deer when moose and whitetail ranges overlapped. Fortunately, moose are now building immunity to the effects of the brainworm, as did the white-tailed deer many years ago. Without immunity, moose exposed to the brainworm die from brain infections.

Relationship with Humans: Hunters consider moose one of the greatest trophies, and have therefore endorsed better game laws, more protected land, and careful management. As a result, moose populations throughout the world are increasing. The moose is an important subsistence food for both the Amerindians and the native peoples of Eurasia.

The velvet on this bull's antlers has started to dry, showing that by August the antlers have reached their full size for this year. (Photograph by Leonard Lee Rue III)

The blood-stained antlers of this bull moose in early September show that the velvet has just been rubbed off. (Photograph by Leonard Lee Rue III)

Rocking his antlers from side to side, this huge bull moose is sending an aggressive challenge to a rival. (Photograph by Len Rue Jr.)

When two equally dominant bulls encounter each other, it is a fight to see who will get to do the breeding. The bulls crash together with tons of pressure as each tries to throw his rival off his feet and gore him. (Photograph by Leonard Lee Rue III)

During rutting season, bull moose sniff the cows' urine and then flehmen, testing for the pheromones that indicate their readiness to breed. (Photograph by Leonard Lee Rue III)

A cow and her four-month-old calf take to the water to feed. Only a few days after birth, calves are able to sample the same vegetation their mothers eat, and they are usually weaned by three months. (Photograph by Leonard Lee Rue III)

These two-month-old twin moose calves still have the russet-red coats they had at birth. (Photograph by Uschi Rue)

By four months of age, moose calves have changed to a dark brown coloration. (Photograph by Leonard Lee Rue III)

Caribou/Reindeer

Range: There is a single species of *Rangifer tarandus* and seven subspecies. In Eurasia the animals are referred to as reindeer, while in North America they are known as caribou. North America caribou emigrated from Asia thousands of years ago, crossing over the Bering Land Bridge during the interglacial periods. At one time, when the world was colder, these animals were found much farther south than their present range. Fossil remains found in Alabama and the preponderance of their inclusion in cave paintings in southern France attest to this fact.

Today reindeer are found all across Eurasia north of the 50th parallel. The 50th parallel is roughly the southern reach of caribou in North America with a few exceptions, such as the Selkirk herd in Idaho, which is endangered. Most caribou spend their lives in the tundra, migrating into boreal forests during winter. Some caribou live in forests or on mountains all year long, while the white Peary's caribou live on the tundra all year.

Description: Basically, caribou are larger than reindeer, but as a species these animals vary in size with a head and body length from 46.8 to 85.8 inches (1,200 and 2,200 mm). They have a tail length of 2.7 to 8.1 inches (70 to 210 mm). They have a shoulder height of between 33.9 and 54.6 inches (870 and 1,400 mm), and weigh between 132 and 700 pounds (60 and 315 kg).

These animals have stocky bodies and stout legs. They are cursorial animals that seemingly can trot forever, although they do gallop when they need extra speed. They have wide, outcurving hooves that can be flared broadly to give support to their body weight. Their dewclaws are long and touch the ground, making an overall square track pattern. The tracks measure roughly 6 by 6 inches (152 by 152 mm) or 36 square inches (23,226 sq. mm). This coverage gives a 500-pound (227 kg) caribou approximately 3.5 pounds (2 kg) of bearing surface to the square inch (25 sq. mm), allowing the animal to walk on soft ground or snow without sinking. In the winter, the soft frog of the caribou's hoof dries and shrinks, making the inside of the hooves concave, which greatly increases the bearing surface. Caribou and reindeer can seemingly float over wet tundra in which a human would bog down.

Caribou and reindeer have only one annual coat. The basic color is a mouse gray, which starts to grow in May as bleached-out hair is sloughed off. In September, adult bulls get a pure white cape, with long hairs hanging below the neck and a wide, white sidestripe that extends to their flanks; they also have a white rump patch. Peary's caribou have an all-white coat. The winter coat, when fully grown, has air-filled guard hairs that are 1.5 to 2 inches (38 to 51 mm) long. In between the guard hairs is a dense woolly undercoat. A caribou/reindeer coat is one of the warmest in the world.

Caribou and reindeer are the only members of the deer family in which both male and female grow antlers. The female's antlers are much smaller and more spindly than the male's. Adult males usually start to grow new antlers in April and lose them in December. Females start antler growth in June and carry antlers until spring. The purpose of the doe's antlers is to repulse young males, which also keep antlers until spring and which try to usurp the vegetation from which the does have laboriously pawed away the snow.

Adult bulls' antlers are bifurcated, with the brow tine expanding to become a palmated shovel. Above the shovel, the antlers sweep back and then forward, having a number of tines and perhaps lacking palmation.

A peculiarity for which caribou are famous is the clicking sound the animals make while walking. It is caused by the tendons slipping over the bones in the animal's foot and serves to keep the animals in contact with each other when they move at night.

This species has broad muzzles because they are primarily grazing animals. They are the only members of the deer family whose rhinarium is completely covered with hair, as a protection against the bitter cold. They have large tarsal, preorbital, and interdigital glands.

Habits: Caribou and reindeer eat grasses; forbs; reeds; sedges; berries and berry bushes; the leaves and twig tips of willow, birch, and aspen; fungi; mosses; and evergreens. One of their dietary mainstays is the white,

Caribou can trot for hours on end. (Photograph by Leonard Lee Rue III)

Map of caribou range in North America

Map of reindeer range in Eurasia

brittle "reindeer moss," a lichen that is exceedingly high in protein.

Because they travel in huge herds, sometimes numbering in the thousands, these animals keep almost constantly on the move. They travel between 11.7 and 34 miles (19 and 55 km) per day. Some herds make a 1,600-mile (2,574 km) round trip between their winter and summer ranges and back again. In winter they break into much smaller groups so they don't have to move as much to find food.

When caribou and reindeer are walking, they do so with their heads lowered, which gives them a dejected look. When trotting, the head is held high with the nose pointing straight forward. Big bulls lay their antlers back alongside their bodies. Caribou and reindeer trot at about 8 miles per hour (14 kmh), and they can keep up this pace seemingly forever. When trotting, they raise their feet high, horizontal to the ground, which enables them to clear the dwarf shrubs of the tundra. They can gallop at over 35 miles per hour (56 kmh).

When frightened or startled, caribou and reindeer often rear up almost vertically in the "excitation jump," which deposits scent from their interdigital glands on the ground. The scent serves as a warning of potential danger to every caribou that passes that way over the next couple of days.

Caribou and reindeer feed on the run. They trot along, stop for a mouthful of vegetation, and trot on again. The animals actually stop to eat from about 6 to 8 A.M. They lie down for a while to chew their cud and then they are off again. Many times caribou will retrace their steps so that they feed again in the same general area, although not in the exact same spot as they did previously. During summer, caribou feed at any time because it does not get dark at night in the Arctic.

Also during summer, they seek out remnant patches of snow to lie on, in order to keep cool and to reduce insect activity. They frequent high ridges, if any are in their area, or go down to the seashore, where strong winds give them relief from flies and mosquitoes. When traveling, caribou and reindeer often follow single-file in parallel lines along trails that have been used for thousands of years.

Communication: Caribou and reindeer are not very vocal. The only sounds I've heard the bulls and cows make is a low, coughing grunt. The calves, when separated from their mothers, make a bawling bleat.

These animals do, however, make extensive use of body language. Cows urge their young to follow by facing the calves and bobbing their heads up and down. Bulls challenge each other also by head bobbing, which causes their dark face to break up the pattern of their white capes. Bulls also thrash bushes and deposit scent on branches, and the clicking sound of their feet is heard at all times.

Breeding: Peak breeding season occurs in mid-October. Each adult bull will try to gather a harem of ten to twelve cows. In the four weeks devoted to the rut, the migration basically stops. Battles between adult bulls are frequent. Occasionally bulls lock antlers and, unable to pull apart, die of starvation, stress, and dehydration. Between fighting and breeding, the fat that bulls accumulated during late summer is soon used up, and many bulls go into winter gaunt and wounded.

Birth and Young: The gestation period for caribou and reindeer is usually 228 days, with most calves dropped between May 15 and June 15. Prior to giving birth, cows go to traditional calving grounds. Each cow separates from the herd to give birth in a secluded area, to prevent her calf from imprinting on another cow. Barren-ground caribou usually have a single calf, while woodland caribou often have twins. Reindeer usually give birth to singletons. Calves have an unspotted, soft-brown coat, and weigh between 10 and 20 pounds (5 and 9 kg).

Caribou and reindeer calves are able to stand in minutes, walk well within an hour, outrun a person in twenty-four hours, and run as fast as their mothers within a week. This precociousness is an essential survival trait for migratory animals.

By four months of age, little bulls have antler growth of several inches. These young bulls are capable of breeding, but are prevented from doing so by the adult bulls. Females reach sexual maturity and can be bred at seventeen months of age.

A domesticated reindeer lived to be twenty years, two months old.

In spring, the caribou's bleached-out hair begins to slough off and new hair begins to grow. Caribou and reindeer cows also start to grow antlers; they are the only females in the *Cervidae* family to do so. (Photograph by Len Rue Jr.)

Enemies: Wolves are the number-one predator, but bears, tigers, and lynx also prey upon caribou and reindeer.

Caribou and reindeer are plagued by hordes of biting, blood-sucking black flies and mosquitoes. They are bedeviled by nose bots and warble flies. The adult warble fly lays eggs on the hair on the animal's legs. The larvae that hatch out enter the bloodstream and migrate to the animal's back. There, in the area between the muscle and the skin, they develop into grubs about 1-inch (25-mm) in length, and get their nourishment from the animal's blood. When fully developed, they cut a hole through the skin and drop to the ground, where they burrow and emerge one year later as adult flies. I have seen caribou skins with more than 400 warble scars, bearing mute testimony to the agony the animal endured.

Relationship with Humans: Hundreds of thousands of reindeer have been domesticated and are herded by native people all across Eurasia. The caribou has never been domesticated. Reindeer have been imported into Alaska, but each venture has failed because the native peoples there are hunters, not herders. There are a few domesticated reindeer herds in both Alaska and Canada. There are also wild herds, which are detrimental to caribou if they interbreed, as the reindeer is a smaller animal.

I have never seen or heard of a caribou showing aggression to humans. Reindeer, which have been domesticated and have lost their fear of people, can be very aggressive.

This woodland caribou bull will cross many rivers along its migration route in Quebec, Canada. (Photograph by Leonard Lee Rue III)

A barren-ground caribou herd crosses an Alaskan river during migration. The animals walk with their heads down. They also eat on the move, pausing only to snatch a bite of vegetation before taking off again. (Photograph by Leonard Lee Rue III)

A bachelor herd of barren-ground caribou in migration, just prior to rutting season. (Photograph by Leonard Lee Rue III)

Right: This bull has removed all but a few of the basal strips of velvet from his antlers. (Photograph by Leonard Lee Rue III)

Below: The residual blood from the just-shed velvet has stained red the antlers of this bull. (Photograph by Leonard Lee Rue III)

Left: This bull thrashes his antlers against a bush to help remove the velvet. (Photograph by Leonard Lee Rue III)

Below: The velvet on this caribou bull's antlers has dried and is just starting to peel. All of the *Cervidae* north of the 35th parallel shed their velvet around September 1. (Photograph by Leonard Lee Rue III)

Above: Caribou calves are on their feet following their mothers within minutes after birth. (Photograph by Len Rue Jr.)

Right: The coat on this three-month-old caribou calf is already changing to its dark coloration. (Photograph by Uschi Rue)

Left: This grizzly bear is covering a barren-ground caribou it has killed. The bear will stay in the area and feed on the carcass until it is consumed. (Photograph by Len Rue Jr.)

An introduced reindeer herd, which has gone wild, migrates in Alaska. (Photograph by Uschi Rue)

Roe Deer

Range: There are two species of roe deer. *Capreolus capreolus* is found in most of Europe as far east as the Volga River in Russia and south to northeastern Iran. *Capreolus pygargus* is found from the Don River in Russia eastward across Siberia to Korea, and south to central China.

Description: These deer are cold-adapted, on par with caribou and moose, but they are also able to occupy a great diversity of habitats. The eastern roe deer is larger than the western. The two species average between 37 and 58.8 inches (950 to 1,510 mm) in head and body length and have a tail length of .625 to 1.5 inches (20 to 40 mm). The extremely short tail and shortened ears are a response to Allen's Rule, which states that the farther north a creature is found, the shorter its extremities will be, to prevent freezing. These deer stand between 25.3 and 39 inches (650 and 1,000 mm) high at the shoulder, and weigh between 33 and 110 pounds (15 to 50 kg).

The summer coat of roe deer is reddish-brown, the ears are black-rimmed, and the underparts are light tan. There is a ring of black around the nose, extending to the corners of the mouth. The winter coat is dark grayish-brown with two white throat patches. While the European roe deer has a white rump patch only during winter, the Siberian roe deer has one year-round. The patch can be flared when the deer is excited or frightened.

The antlers of the European roe buck average about 7 inches (178 mm) in length, and have three tines to each side, a large burr or rosette, and heavy perlation. The antlers of the Siberian roe buck can grow up to 15 inches (381 mm) in length, have five to six times per side, a small rosette, and little perlation.

Roe bucks are unique in that they are the only deer to grow antlers during winter. The reason is that the roe deer's breeding season occurs during summer, and bucks must be prepared to battle. Antlers are cast in October and November, a trait similar to pronghorn antelope. Occasionally some does grow small antlers.

These deer have forehead, preorbital, and metatarsal scent glands. They have interdigital glands on only their hind feet. In scraping, they use their front feet to make the scrape, then stamp the scrape with their hind feet to deposit scent—something most other deer do not do.

Habits: Roe deer are creatures of dense forest wherever possible. In some areas, human activities have forced these deer to adapt to more open areas. They sometimes are seen feeding in small herds in such areas, but even there each animal keeps space between itself and its cohorts. In the forest, males are solitary, and except for their current fawns, females are also solitary.

Roe deer are territorial. Each female has a small territory for which she will fight and from which she will drive all other females, except her immediate young. Males have larger territories, overlapping those of two or three females, but they stay away from does, except during rutting season.

As forest creatures, roe deer are saltatorial runners, bounding away for a short distance and then hiding. Roe deer are not fast runners, nor do they have much endurance. They may stot when first starting to run. Most often, when disturbed, the deer simply remain motionless and let the danger walk by, or else they slink off, taking advantage of all available cover. They may also take to water, as they are strong swimmers.

Roe deer do best in a succession forest—land being reclaimed by a forest after fire, flood, or lumbering has removed most of the mature trees, and a profusion of brush is growing back. Such areas offer the greatest concealment and the greatest diversity of food. Roe deer feed upon grasses, forbs, leaves, tender twig tops, fruits, berries and berry bushes, lichens, fungi, acorns, and beechnuts. Almost all roe deer live close to agricultural areas and avidly eat farm crops of all kinds.

Communication: The most commonly heard call of the roe deer is the sharp, high-pitched alarm bark that is given by both sexes. Bucks also bark when challeng-

Roe deer, such as this female, seldom stray far from the dark forests in which they live. (Photograph by Leonard Lee Rue III)

Map of roe deer range in Eurasia

ing rival males. Does give a low-pitched whistle when they are trying to locate fawns that may have moved between nursing periods. The young have a bleat when calling the doe and a high-pitched scream when they are frightened or being attacked.

Roe deer bucks mark overhead branches with scent from their forehead and preorbital glands. They hook bushes and saplings with their antlers, leaving both visual and olfactory signals. They make scrapes around the perimeter of their territories in which they deposit scent, urine, and feces. Roe deer do not self-advertise by urinating on themselves.

Breeding: Roe deer have a summer rutting season, which allows bucks to replenish their fat stores long before winter. Delayed implantation allows the female to be impregnated at this time, yet not give birth until spring. The fertile blastocyst will float loose in the doe's uterus for about four months before attaching itself to the uterine wall. (This is the standard fertilization procedure for bears and occurs with most members of the weasel family, but the roe deer is the only member of the deer family in which it takes place.)

Yearling does are forced out of their mother's territory before she gives birth to new fawns. Acquiring a territory is paramount to the survival of all deer. Young does can stay only if part of the buck's territory is not already claimed by a mature doe.

The actual breeding takes place in July and August, with bucks attending just the estrus doe. Vicious fights occur when a rival male invades a resident buck's territory in search of an estrus doe. There are long courtship chases in which the doe runs in circles; sometimes the circles are small and may be just around a bush. In an open field, the circle may be 50 feet (15 m) across, and the grass or grain may be stamped down completely. Old-time European farmers called these circles "fairy rings."

Females that don't breed or don't conceive in the summer may come in estrus again in November and December and, for such does, there is no delayed implantation.

Birth and Young: In late November or December, the blastocysts of the does that were bred during the summer attach themselves to the walls of the uterus, and development of the fetus proceeds. The gestation period is approximately 150 days, with fawns born in May or June. Adult does usually give birth to twins and occasionally to triplets. Fawns have bright, russet-red coats with three horizontal rows of white spots on each side of the body. At birth, fawns weigh about 3.75 pounds (2 kg).

The doe keeps the fawns hidden in separate locations. She stays away from them, but remains in the general area. She will return to nurse them three to five times in a twenty-four-hour period. The fawns are kept hidden for ten to twelve days and are then strong enough to follow after their mother. They will stay with her for about a year, when they will be forced to leave to find a territory of their own.

The oldest recorded age for a roe deer is seventeen years.

Enemies: Roe deer are preyed upon by domestic and feral dogs, wolves, bears, wolverines, lynx, tigers, and even wild pigs. Most folks are amazed to learn that wild pigs relish meat and will consume every fawn they can locate.

Relationship with Humans: Because there are few truly wild places left in Europe, the roe deer is one of the most intensively studied and managed of all game animals. It is hunted extensively and is to European hunters what the white-tailed deer is to hunters in North America. Due to the interest in and management of this deer, its future is bright.

GLOSSARY

bachelor group: A group of deer composed exclusively of males. The male members of most of the *Cervidae* group together and live apart from the females and young except during rutting, or breeding, season or when both sexes are forced to occupy the same area that has food during the winter.

cursorial: Having the long legs needed for running. All members of the deer family are considered to be cursorial animals.

dewclaws: Two shrunken hooves located behind the main hooves. All members of the deer family have just four toes; they lack what would be our thumb or big toe. The toes corresponding to our own middle and ring fingers are their two main hooves; the dewclaws are the toes corresponding to our index and pinky fingers.

dimorphism: Existence of two different forms within a species. Because the males of most members of the *Cervidae* are so much larger in body size than are the females, the species are said to be dimorphic.

estrus period: The time during which any female mammal can be made pregnant. In *Cervidae* this period is of short duration and usually lasts just twenty-four to twenty-eight hours. It is during the estrus period that the female ovulates, discharging eggs from her ovaries into her uterus, where they can be fertilized if she is bred by the male. If during that time span she is not bred or does not conceive, the female goes out of estrus but has another period twenty-eight days later.

forehead glands: Sudoriferous scent glands in the forehead skin. (See accompanying photo.) Many members of the *Cervidae*, both male and female, have them. The animals make chemical signposts by rubbing these glands against weeds or saplings, depositing their individual scent thereon. Males have far more such glands than do females, and the glands become much more active prior to and during rutting season.

guard hairs: The longer, stronger, outer hair that protects the softer, finer undercoat of most members of the *Cervidae*.

inguinal glands: Scent glands that lie between the hind legs of some deer. They have been discovered so recently that little is known about them or the role they play in chemical communication.

interdigital glands: Scent glands located between the toes that emit scent as the deer walks and help one deer track another. (See accompanying photo.)

maxillary canine teeth: Primitive upper teeth in some *Cervidae*, located in front of the pre-molars. In Chinese water deer, such teeth may be as long as 3 inches (76 mm), while in some white-tailed deer they may not even protrude above the gum line. Most deer species do not have these teeth.

metatarsal glands: Glands located on the hind legs between the knee and the foot of some deer species. (See accompanying photo.) These are glands that are atrophying in the deer that have them; they apparently serve no useful purpose today.

nasal glands: Glands found just inside the nasal passageway of deer. (See accompanying photo.) There is very little known about the function or importance of these particular glands.

palmated: Appearing flattened like the palm of a hand, with points or tines projecting from the forward edge like fingers. The antlers of adult bull moose and fallow deer are typically palmated, as are the "shovels" or brow tines of caribou and reindeer. Occasionally any deer species may have a palmation of the main beams.

pedicles: Bony protrusions that grow on the frontal skull plate of the *Cervidae* and form the base from which the antlers will grow. The pedicles form on the skull where a special layer of tissue called the periosteum has been laid down. Muntjacs have the longest pedicles of any deer.

photoperiodism: The response to the amount of daylight in a twenty-four-hour period. One of the greatest forces governing the activities of most living things in the world, it is the force that determines, with an exactness, when birds and animals migrate, breed, give birth, go into hibernation, and emerge from hibernation in the spring. In mammals and birds, the amount of daylight is picked up through the eyes via the optic nerve, which sends electrical impulses to the pineal gland. This gland, located within the brain, in turn sends chemical signals to the pituitary gland, which causes the endocrine system to send hormones through the body via the bloodstream that either speed up or slow down body functions.

preorbital glands: Gland located in the forward corner of all deer's eyes. (See accompanying photo.) Also known as the tear duct or lachrymal gland, this gland gives off a scent that the animals often deposit on vegetation or wood by rubbing. Some of the *Cervidae* expose the scent molecules to the air by widely flaring the gland open.

preputial gland: Gland that has been found in the skin at the tip of the white-tailed buck's penis sheath. It is not understood just what purpose this gland serves.

salivary glands: Glands that excrete saliva, which are located at the top of the mouth in male *Cervidae*. The flow of saliva increases dramatically during rutting season. The more sexually active the male, the more he drips or drools.

saltatorial running: A bounding type of locomotion that requires the animals to have large, powerful haunches.

The forehead (1), preorbital (2), and nasal glands (3). (Photograph by Leonard Lee Rue III)

The tarsal (4) and metatarsal glands (5). (Photograph by Leonard Lee Rue III)

stotting: The type of locomotion wherein all of the animal's four feet leave the ground at the same time. It is an adaptation to allow the animals to quickly ascend steep hillsides. Many *Cervidae* stot occasionally; however, none stot all the time as it is extremely energy intensive.

tarsal glands: Scent gland located inside a deer's foot at the juncture of the tibia, or main leg bone, and the tarsus (corresponding to our ankle). (See photo on page 153.) The subaceous and sudoriferous glands beneath the skin are connected to hair follicles—ducts bringing secretions through the skin to long tufts of hair. The secretions have no odor, but they do have fatty lipids that hold the urine deposited on the hair by the deer. Bacterial action on the lipids and urine produces the strong musky odor for which this gland is noted. Both males and females rub-urinate on these glands. The more dominant the animal, the more frequently it urinates on the tarsal glands and the darker the hair around the glands will be.

Tenuis: The parasitic meningeal worm or "brainworm." The full Latin name is *Parelaphostrongylus tenuis*. It is carried by the white-tailed deer, which have built up immunity to it. However, the deer release the larval stage of these worms, passing from their bodies with their feces. These larvae infect snails and slugs, which in turn are eaten by other deer, such as elk, moose, and mule deer. The ingested larvae penetrate the abomasum and get into the bloodstream, migrate to the animal's spinal column, and after further incubation, to the brain. Animals that have not built up immunity develop infected brains, which causes a loss of motor control and eventually results in death.

tines: The bony outgrowths of antlers projecting from the main beam.

tusks: Another name for the long, downward curving canine teeth that some *Cervidae* have.

A herd of barren-ground caribou crosses a river during migration. (Photograph by Leonard Lee Rue III)

This two-week-old white-tailed fawn is super alert, as shown by the high head posture. (Photograph by Leonard Lee Rue III)

Peeling velvet decorates the antlers of this barren-ground caribou. (Photograph by Leonard Lee Rue III)

BIBLIOGRAPHY

Brown, Robert D., ed. *The Biology of Deer*. New York: Springer-Verlag, 1991.

Byers, C. Randall, and George A. Bettas, eds. *Records of North American Big Game*. 11th ed. Missoula, MT: Boone & Crockett Club, 1999.

Caton, John Dean. *The Antelope and Deer of North America*. Cambridge, MA: Hurd & Houghton, 1877.

Clutten-Brock, T. H., F. E. Guiness, and S. D. Albon. *Red Deer*. Chicago, IL: University of Chicago Press, 1982.

DeNahlik, A. J. *Wild Deer*. Southampton, England: Ashford Press Publishers, 1987.

Franzmann, Albert W., and Charles C. Schwartz, eds. *Ecology and Management of the North American Moose*. Washington, DC: Smithsonian Institution Press, 1998.

Geist, Valerius. *Deer of the World*. Mechanicsburg, PA: Stackpole Books, 1998.

——. *Elk Country*. Minocqua, WI: North Wind Press, Inc., 1991.

——. *Moose*. Stillwater, MN: Voyageur Press, 1999.

——. *Mule Deer Country*. Minocqua, WI: North Wind Press, Inc., 1990.

——. *Whitetail Tracks*. Iola, WI: Krause Publications, 2001.

Gerlach, Duane, Sally Atwater, Judith Schnell, eds. *Deer*. Mechanicsburg, PA: Stackpole Books, 1994.

Kalle, Lowell K., ed. *White-tailed Deer: A Wildlife Management Institute Book*.

Harrisburg, PA: Stackpole Books, 1984.

Peterson, Randolph L. *North American Moose*. Toronto: University of Toronto Press, 1955.

Putnam, Rory. *The Natural History of Deer*. Ithaca, NY: Cornell University Press, 1988.

Rue III, Leonard Lee. *The Complete Guide to Game Animals*. New York: Outdoor Life Books, 1968.

——. *The Deer of North America*. New York: Outdoor Life Books, 1978.

——. *Leonard Lee Rue III's Way of the Whitetail*. Stillwater, MN: Voyageur Press, 2000.

——. *The World of the White-tailed Deer*. Philadelphia: J. B. Lippincott, 1962.

Schaller, George B. *The Deer & the Tiger*. Chicago: University of Chicago Press, 1967.

Tate, G. H. H. *Mammals of Eastern Asia*. New York: The Macmillan Co., 1947.

Thomas, Jack Ward, and Dale E. Toweill, eds. *Elk of North America: A Wildlife Management Institute Book*. Harrisburg, PA: Stackpole Books, 1982.

Wallmo, Olaf C., ed. *Mule and Black-tailed Deer of North America: A Wildlife Management Institute Book*. Lincoln, NE: University of Nebraska Press, 1981.

Whitaker Jr., John D., and William Hamilton Jr. *Mammals of the Eastern United States*. Ithaca, NY: Cornell University Press, 1998.

Whitehead, G. Kenneth. *Deer of the World*. New York: The Viking Press, 1972.

——. *The Whitehead Encyclopedia of Deer*. Stillwater, MN: Voyageur Press, 1993.

Yurgenson, P. B., ed. *Studies on Mammals in Government Preserves*.

Translated from the Russian. Washington, DC: National Science Foundation, 1961.

INDEX

ABOUT THE AUTHOR

Dr. Leonard Lee Rue III has spent much of his life studying, photographing, and living with wildlife in its natural habitats. The most published wildlife photographer in North America, he is also the author of twenty-eight books, including *How I Photograph Wildlife, The Deer of North America,* and *Way of the Whitetail.* He writes monthly columns for *Deer & Deer Hunting* and the online magazine *www.vividlight.com.*

He received the 1987 Outdoor Writers Association of America's "Excellence in Craft" Award. In 1990 he received an honorary doctorate of science from Colorado State University, for "the dissemination of knowledge on wildlife," and in 1997 he received a Lifetime Achievement Award from the North American Nature Photographer's Association (NANPA).

In addition to his work as a writer and photographer, Dr. Rue conducts lectures and seminars throughout the country on white-tailed deer, turkey, and nature photography. He also produces photographic, instructional, educational, and nature videos.

Dr. Rue and his wife Uschi own and operate Leonard Rue Video Productions, Inc., which supplies top-quality stock video footage covering the complete realm of wildlife and nature subjects. With his son, Len Rue Jr., Dr. Rue also owns Leonard Rue Enterprises, a photo stock agency and online store.

Leonard Rue Enterprises Stock Photo Agency supplies top-quality wildlife and nature photography—both color transparencies and black-and-white prints—to advertising and editorial markets worldwide. The L.L.Rue online store offers a unique line of photographic equipment and accessories for the discriminating photographer and outdoor enthusiast. For more information please contact:

Leonard Rue Video Productions, Inc. (www.ruevideo.com) and/or Leonard Rue Enterprises, Inc. (www.rue.com), 138 Millbrook Road, Blairstown, NJ, 07825-9534, or call 1-800-734-2568.